An architectural guide

•••

Thom Gorst
Photographs by Keith Collie

Bath

An architectural guide

an ● ● ● ellipsis publication

• • •

British Library Cataloguing in Publication
A CIP record for this book is available from the British Library

Bath: an architectural guide

FIRST EDITION 1997
PUBLISHER Ellipsis London Limited
ADDRESS 55 Charlotte Road London EC2A 3QT
E MAIL ellipsis@cityscape.co.uk
WWW http://www.gold.net/ellipsis
COPYRIGHT © 1997 Ellipsis London Limited
ISBN 1 899858 28 8
SERIES EDITOR Tom Neville
EDITOR Annie Bridges
DESIGN Jonathan Moberly
LAYOUT Pauline Harrison
PRINTING AND BINDING Hong Kong

Contents

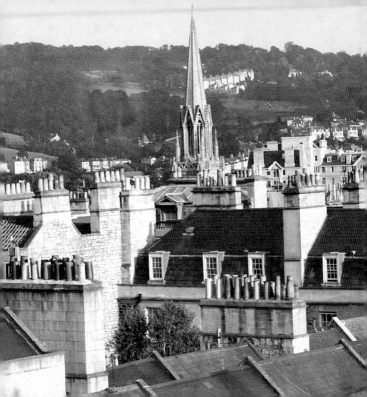

Introduction

The city of Bath sits in a bowl of the hills at the southern tip of the Cotswolds, at a point where the River Avon forms a loop around a short peninsula. It was here that the Romans established their city of Aquae Sulis, and it was here too that eighteenth-century English society life settled in the refined luxury of the architecture we now call 'Georgian'. This term needs some explanation: it is not that the British monarchy actually dictated the direction architecture should take, but simply that the throne happened to be occupied by someone called George from 1714 to 1830. And since the great squares, crescents and terraces of Bath were built in the hundred years between 1725 and 1825, the term Georgian is a perfectly adequate description for them. This is the architecture that gives this comparatively small city its international reputation.

The built scenery is dramatic. When viewed from one of the hilltop vantage points (the best is on North Hill to the south-east), the light golden local stone seems to be everywhere, relieved only by the green roofs of the Snowhill Housing Estate on the east side and the blue gas holders to the west. Almost all of what we see before us dates from after 1725.

THE ROMAN CITY

The popular version of Bath's history before the Romans belongs in the realm of myth. A Prince Bladud, son of the King of Britain, contracted leprosy and lived in isolation as a swineherd. Somewhere near Bath, his pigs (who by now had also caught the disease) started to roll in muddy water, and as a result were cured. The rehabilitated Bladud returned to his father and founded the city of Bath.

It is a fact that the comparatively small Roman city of Aquae Sulis, named after the Celtic goddess of hot springs, was established to take advantage of the healing power of the Mendip water. Its sole function was that of a resort – it had virtually no administrative power – but as such it was extremely popular, attracting visitors from all over the northern Empire. It was situated on the Roman Fosse Way, which linked north-east Britain with the south-west, and it has been claimed that it was easier to get to Bath in Roman times than at any other time up until the end of the eighteenth century.

Roman Bath is now visible only in the spectacular remains within the Baths complex and in the alignment of the principal streets within the city walls.

FROM ROMAN TO GEORGIAN

The Roman city declined and was finally overrun by English invaders in the sixth century AD. Dark times followed, and we do not get a clear picture of organised civic life until the Middle Ages, when Bath prospered thanks to the wool and cloth trade which was well established throughout the region. Before the dissolution of the monasteries in the 1530s, the city also had a powerful priory, with up to 40 monks. The present abbey stands on the site of their church, which was considerably larger.

Very little of the fabric of the medieval city survives. The present abbey structure was started at the end of the fifteenth century but not completed until the nineteenth century. Except for a few isolated fragments of the medieval walls, the only significant survivor from these times is St Mary Magdalen Church in Holloway, a one-time chapel and leper house that also dates from the end of the fifteenth century.

Apart from these, the earliest remnants of Bath's architectural history are the merchants' houses of the first decades of the eighteenth century, the period that immediately predates the massive social and architectural expansion of the Georgian era.

Bath: an architectural guide

THE GEORGIAN CITY

Powerful patrons helped to establish Bath's early reputation as a resort. Anne of Denmark visited the healing springs in 1616, and Charles II arrived in 1663 on a quest for a cure for his wife's sterility. But in the seventeenth century the principal trade of the city was still wool, and the baths were unpleasant in the extreme.

By 1695, however, the famous traveller Celia Fiennes was able to record that 'The town and all its accommodations is adapted to the batheing [sic] and drinking of the waters and to nothing else.' The increasing prosperity and stability enjoyed by the country's privileged classes had prompted them to seek a resort where they could meet together in the summer months, leaving behind the intolerable atmosphere of London.

In 1702 and 1703 Queen Anne visited the city to take the waters. The following year, the gambler Richard 'Beau' Nash became Master of Ceremonies and presided over the spectacular transformation of Bath from a spa town to a fashionable social resort. He organised improvements in the public utilities, including the provision of street paving and lighting; he established a new Assembly Room in North Parade (now demolished); and he laid down a strict code of etiquette, which forbade duelling and the wearing of swords and riding boots by gentlemen, and of white aprons – associated at the time with prostitution – by the ladies.

Another key figure of this boom period was Ralph Allen, who derived his wealth from reorganising the postal system. He then bought the stone quarries in Combe Down and vigorously marketed the material far and wide. His great house at Prior Park was a magnificent advertisement for Bath stone; it was also visited by many of the greatest names in early eighteenth-century English culture.

The architecture that housed the social élite during their visits to the city was largely the creation of John Wood the Elder and Younger. Wood the Elder settled in Bath in 1727 after having worked in London, where he had acquired a knowledge of Palladian design. Inigo Jones, who had studied Palladio's work in the Veneto and imported his ideas to Britain, had completed London's first square at Covent Garden less than a century earlier. Wood was certainly aware of this, and of the succession of squares built in the capital in the late seventeenth century.

While in Yorkshire in 1725 Wood started to develop an interest in the opportunities for fashionable urban expansion that were beginning to appear in Bath. Using a city plan he had sent up to him, he spent his spare time preparing designs for huge developments in the city. According to his own famous account, 'I proposed to make a grand Place of Assembly, to be called the Royal Forum of Bath; another Place, no less magnificent, for the Exhibition of Sports, to be called the Grand Circus; and a third Place, of equal State with either of the former, for the Practice of medicinal Exercises, to be called the Imperial Gymnasium of the City.' Wood consciously drew on the forms of Rome to create the magnificent sequence of urban spaces for which he will best be remembered.

After a very vigorous promotion of his ideas, and some false starts, Wood decided to begin his development with Queen Square to the north-west of the old city. The project was initiated in 1728, with Wood both architect and speculator. From here, Gay Street was gradually laid out from the north-east corner. This led to the Circus, begun in 1754 and completed by Wood's son after his death in the same year. The younger Wood laid out Brock Street from the west of the Circus in 1764; it was designed to be a low-key approach to the spatially magnificent Royal Crescent of 1767.

The elder Wood's 'Royal Forum' of Bath was started in 1739, but never finished. Only The Parades were completed, which were to have been the Forum's north side.

The buildings which grouped together to form the city's grand urban spaces were in fact rows of speculative housing. Behind many of Bath's uniform façades lie houses built by different builders to different designs. Often, the key architects established only the basic design rules for a development, and then leased individual units (called 'messuages') to smaller builders. It was the façades that unified the urban spaces and guaranteed to the landowners that the proposed development would be of a particular standard. The following extracts are from a typical lease granted to a builder called Samuel Palmer for the construction of a house in the Royal Crescent:

> [Palmer] shall and will erect and build one substantial stone and timber messuage or tenement ... which house shall in front cover the whole breadth of the ground conveyed, and shall set out and build the front wall thereof [the façade] in and upon such line as shall be marked out by the sd John Wood ... so as such line shall cause the front of such messuage to range and be in an uniform line with the whole pile of building intended to be called the Royal Crescent ... [he shall] finish and make the same messuage of the same height and of the like ornaments in front only as the west front of the messuage or tenement lately built by the sd Thos Brock at the east end of the sd Crescent.

Bath has many examples of the lack of uniformity in housing design that existed before Wood started his work. Many of the street frontages of these early houses have gabled upper floors and sash windows (these were introduced around 1700) surrounded by heavily moulded architraves. Surviving examples from the period 1700 to 1725 can be found in Green Street and Broad Street and Chapel Court. 'General Wolfe's House' in Trim Street and 'General Wade's House' in the Abbey Church Yard are both from the 1720s, and display early attempts to organise their façades into a Palladian discipline. Also belonging to the pre-Wood era in form, if not in fact, is the curious Rosewell House in Kingsmead Square of 1736. This is so unrestrained in its ornamentation that Wood called it 'piratical'. Compare such examples with the quiet restraint of, say, Wood's South Parade, and the revolution he brought about becomes clear. Instead of individual houses that made little attempt to relate to their neighbours, Wood took the model of Palladio's great merchants' palazzi in Vicenza, as imported into Britain by Inigo Jones, and established it as an enduring format for British speculative housing.

GEORGIAN ARCHITECTURE AFTER THE WOODS

The period of vigorous housebuilding which began with the north side of Queen Square lasted until the beginning of the nineteenth century. These years provided a good deal of variety in the detailed design of the type. For example, there were different ways in which builders dealt with the city's contours. Some developments, like the great crescents (Royal and Camden), follow the contours – Lansdown Crescent in particular positively celebrates the contour with its graceful meander. Other terraces cut across the contours, however. The master of this was John Pinch the Elder, whose subtle ways of stepping the composition down the hill provided a fitting finale to this chapter of Bath's development.

Another change as the century progressed was the increasing need, for economic reasons, to build housing of four storeys above the ground. It

Bath: an architectural guide

was not easy to shoehorn such a block into a convincing Palladian composition, especially when the architect tried to use pediments to create a palace-like form. At Northumberland Buildings, for instance, the top storey seems to squash what is below, rendering Thomas Baldwin's delicate ornamentation quite redundant. At Norfolk Crescent, the pediment is curiously disengaged from the main cornice by the top storey, while at New Sydney Place the pediments in the centre and at the ends add little to the overall composition.

Most of these developments date from the end of the great Georgian era. By the end of the eighteenth century, Bath's exclusiveness had disappeared. Jane Austen's first visit to the city was in 1797, when she stayed at no. 1 The Paragon. From 1800 to 1805 she lived at no. 4 Sydney Place, but she was never especially fond of her surroundings. If the fashionable set was not following the Prince Regent to Brighton, then it was crossing the Channel to savour the delights of the Alps. Within 30 years, the railways would arrive.

THE NINETEENTH CENTURY

So dominant is the neo-Palladian housing in the city that the eclecticism of the nineteenth century is pushed into second place.

Two architects in particular represent this period in Bath: Henry Edmund Goodridge (1797–1864) and James Wilson (1816–1900). Goodridge gave us the Italianate Beckford's Tower and the strictly classical Cleveland Bridge, but some of his best work was in the private houses he built on the slopes surrounding the city – Fiesole, which he built in 1848 on Bathwick Hill, is now happily accessible as the Youth Hostel. A walk up Lansdown Hill provides a good showcase of Wilson's talent: St Stephen's Lansdown and St Stephen's Villas, The Royal School and

Kingswood School are all his work and demonstrate the wide range of idioms he was capable of building within.

Bath has little of the grandly confident nineteenth-century commercial architecture that is so plentiful in its larger neighbour, Bristol, and little too of note from the first half of the twentieth century. The bold architecture associated with the two railway lines, the pair of banks at the top of Milsom Street and the delightful façade of St Michael's Church House on Walcot Street are rare representatives of their respective eras.

THE TWENTIETH CENTURY: CONSERVATIONISTS AND DEVELOPERS

The Second World War did not scar Bath as badly as it could have done: in his promise to reach for his gun whenever he heard the word 'culture', Goering was mercifully off-target. The poorer areas down in Kingsmead were the worst hit; the Assembly Rooms were also gutted and some of the set-piece terraces seriously damaged. The key buildings were faithfully rebuilt.

Peacetime destruction was more thorough. In the centre, much of great value was demolished to make way for the Woolworths (now Littlewoods) and Marks & Spencer stores, both in a bland post-war neo-Georgian idiom, while nearby in Southgate, Owen Luder's shopping development raised two fingers to all that Bath offered by means of an architectural heritage. In the south-west of the city, in the heavily bombed district, much more was torn down, to be replaced with even more incredibly insensitive sub-modern blocks. By the time Snailum's Beaufort Hotel (now the Hilton) was completed in the early 1970s, the case against antipathetic modern architecture was complete.

Had it not been for the campaigns staged by preservationists in the 1970s, the city would now look much different. The Buchanan Plan of

1965 had proposed a diversion of the A4 road across the same water-meadows to the east of the city that have recently been scarred forever by a new bypass flyover. It also advocated a traffic tunnel from the Paragon to just below the Royal Crescent. Although never realised, the plan blighted much of the north-eastern approach to the city.

Occasionally, celebrations of out-and-out modernism have emerged, and have been recognised for their quality. Terry Farrell and Nicholas Grimshaw's pioneering plastic shed for Herman Miller on the city's western fringe and Aaron Evans' attractive car showroom just south of the river are both sensitively scaled and contribute to the cityscape.

Otherwise, much contemporary development has sought to (or been constrained to) make some reference to the city's traditional context. Much of quality arose from the positive influence of architect John Darbourne, who as consultant to the city from 1985 to 1990 worked to promote a progressive attitude towards architecture. Notable recent schemes that offer a contemporary architecture which is nevertheless responsive to the context of the city include Feilden Clegg's Cleveland Reach housing and Bridgemead home for the elderly; Nealon Tanner's two schools; Aaron Evans' Seven Dials office/retail scheme; and the new Magistrates Court.

A CITY TO LIVE IN

The drama of the architecture as it weaves around the contours of the hills, and the consistency and beauty of the local stone used as a building material, make Bath one of the most visited cities in the world. Yet as a historical document it is terribly biased. The Pump Room and the Assembly Rooms might be the most popular venues for visitors, but they reveal very little of the life that has been lived within the city.

People believe that in studying the architecture of the terraces and crescents of Bath they are catching an accurate glimpse of life in the eighteenth century. They are not. They are catching a glimpse of how the most privileged section of Bath's society lived. As R W Brunskill pointed out in his famous guide to vernacular architecture, a building's chances of survival depend very much upon its status within society. So it is that we might find an abbey that is 500 years old or a manor house that is 350 years old, but of artisans' dwellings, it is difficult to find any over 200 years old. Much of the fabric in which the majority of Bath's residents lived a century ago has disappeared. Little is said of the prostitutes of Avon Street, or the tinkers of Holloway who lived their own active lives at the same time as Beau Nash or John Wood. Much of their memory has been actively erased by historians who believe that their subject is not concerned with the less fortunate sides of society.

By the same token, today's visitor should be assured that Bath is not just a museum-place of a long-passed social phenomenon. It is a living urban organism, of just about the right size to live in, with – as it happens – a lot of incredible architecture. I love it.

Much of Bath's interesting architecture is centrally placed and can be seen on foot. The city is also reasonably friendly to cyclists, although there is much unwelcome traffic congestion. The hills are not too much of a problem, and only on the most northern terraces will it be necessary to get off and push. Bikes can be hired from the Avon Valley Cyclery beneath Bath Spa railway station.

The guide is divided into geographical sections. The most central part of the city has four sections, with the location details for each entry forming a logical walking tour.

The outer parts of Bath are divided, clockwise, into sections, starting in the north-west with Lansdown Crescent. When a building in another section is nearby, it is noted in the 'Location' details at the foot of the page.

Many of the descriptions refer to compass directions (I always find it useful to carry a small compass on architectural tours). I also recommend taking a small pair of binoculars – not just for seeing distant buildings (like Sham Castle from Parade Gardens) but also for examining details (on the Abbey, for example).

Throughout the guide I have made reference to the following works:
Graham Davis and Penny Bonsall, *Bath: A New History*, 1996
Adam Fergusson and Tim Mowl, *The Sack of Bath – and After*, 1973, extended 1989
Walter Ison, *The Georgian Buildings of Bath*, 2nd. ed. 1980
Neil Jackson, *Nineteenth Century Bath*, 1991
Nikolaus Pevsner, *North Somerset and Bristol*, 1958
Charles Robertson, *Bath: An Architectural Guide*, 1975
Peter Smithson, *Walks Within the Walls*, 1971

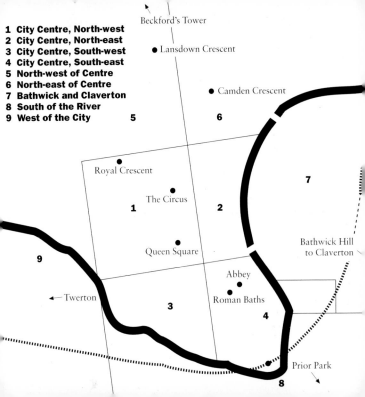

1 **City Centre, North-west**
2 **City Centre, North-east**
3 **City Centre, South-west**
4 **City Centre, South-east**
5 **North-west of Centre**
6 **North-east of Centre**
7 **Bathwick and Claverton**
8 **South of the River**
9 **West of the City**

Beckford's Tower

● Lansdown Crescent

● Camden Crescent

5   6

7

● Royal Crescent

1   The Circus   2

9   ● Queen Square

● Abbey

← Twerton   ● Roman Baths

3   4

Bathwick Hill
to Claverton

Prior Park →

8

City Centre, North-west

Queen Square

Wood's palatial Queen Square was the first of the great sequence of urban spaces that culminated with the Royal Crescent (see page 52) some 40 years later. Wood had been attracted to Bath by the news of its potential for rapid expansion. While working in Yorkshire he had sent for a survey of the city and had produced ambitious plans for its development.

Having had experience of working in London, Wood followed the precedent for the domestic square first established in England one hundred years earlier at Covent Garden's Piazza. Here, the architect Inigo Jones had formed a rectangular open space, just like an Italian piazza, on which two of the sides were fronted by architecturally uniform rows of houses.

Queen Square reflected Wood's desire that places 'for People to assemble together ... ought to be separated from the Ground common to Men and Beasts, and even to Mankind in General, if decency and good order are necessary'. In other words, the new square was to be an exclusive enclosure, cut off from common life.

We know much of Wood's early intentions for the site. It was originally to be levelled, with the north, west and east sides conceived as a 'palace forecourt' intended to be viewed from the south. The north side was to dominate and the south side be built as a 'grand parade' set further back. In the event, Wood was able to save a substantial sum by allowing the natural southerly slope of the ground to remain. He also intended that the east and west sides should be similar to each other, offering complete frontages to the square. As we shall see, the west side was built differently.

Wood obtained leases from the landowner John Gay to start the scheme, and in turn sublet small parcels of land to builders who were to carry out the work in exact accordance with his design. Building began in 1729, and the square was completed seven years later.

John Wood the Elder 1728–36

John Wood the Elder 1728–36

The north side is the grandest. It is, according to Pevsner, 'one of the finest Palladian compositions in England designed before 1730'. Like Palladio, who had published much of his work in his 'Four Books of Architecture' (*Quattro Libri*, 1570), when Wood published his designs he idealised them. A famous drawing of the north side shows some interesting differences from the scheme as built. We can see seven houses on this side of the square. Each has three 'bays' of windows, while the central house has five. In the drawing, each house has been given a central doorway, but in reality the doors had to be set on one side to allow for a large ground-floor room with two windows. The marvellous thing about this new Georgian architecture was that it could accommodate these offset front doors without compromising the design.

Despite being seven separate dwellings, the north side appears to be one building, with emphasis placed in the centre and ends, just like a Palladian palazzo. There is a rusticated base throughout, while the first and second floors are given flat pilasters. At the centre and ends, these pilasters become three-quarter Corinthian columns, which give the impression that the centre and ends stand well in front of the rest. It is a typically Palladian illusion of depth: in reality the façade is almost flat.

The west side was intended to be the same as the east, but was eventually built with a void in the centre. This was the forecourt of a large mansion set further back, which was flanked by two similar pavilions facing the square. The pavilions are still there, but the void was filled by a Greek Revival block by Pinch the Younger in 1830 that was intended to harmonise in its own way with the rest of the square. We must form our own view of how we would prefer it: with a west side matching the east; with the original gap acting as a forecourt to a house set further back; or with the Pinch addition.

John Wood the Elder 1728–36

John Wood the Elder 1728–36

The south side, now a hotel, is more sombre Wood architecture, with a delicately accentuated central part and end bays. The left part of the range has a clinical newness – it was rebuilt after bombing in the Second World War.

The central garden is now more of a public amenity than an architectural asset. It is not as originally planned, and – like the Circus (page 38) and St James's Square (page 170) – the trees and traffic deny an appreciation of the whole. Wood's earliest drawings show it divided by gravel walks into four planted sections, with a basin, complete with obelisk, in the centre. The obelisk was erected by Beau Nash in 1738, and is his homage to Frederick, Prince of Wales.

Queen's Parade, the terrace placed diagonally to the north-west, is by Wood the Younger, 1770, and occupies a site originally intended for the New Assembly Rooms.

LOCATION start of the first central section walk

John Wood the Elder 1728–36

Northumberland Buildings

This is one of the earliest speculative works by Baldwin, who went on to design Somersetshire Buildings in 1782 (page 68), Great Pulteney Street in 1788 (page 232), and the Pump Room in 1791 (page 136). It makes a very interesting comparison with the architecture of nearby Queen Square (page 22), and shows how the Georgian style had evolved in those intense 50 years.

Northumberland Buildings was one of the earliest examples in Bath of the large-scale use of a four-storey domestic elevation. This might have made good economic sense, but it presented architectural problems. Throughout the nineteenth century, many architects struggled to squeeze large, commercially viable buildings into a classical formula. Here, the part of the façade beneath the entablature and three pediments would have been quite satisfactory without the fourth attic storey, which seems to press down on what is below. But Pevsner admired it, calling it a 'very fine broad and tall Adamish composition'. Look especially at the arches over the windows in the central and end elements, and the delicate carved decoration between the first and second floors.

Other, and perhaps more convincing, examples of the four-storey terrace are at Sydney Place (page 238) and Cavendish Crescent (page 176), of 1808 and 1829 respectively, both by Pinch.

LOCATION on the south side of Wood Street; leave Queen Square at the south-west corner
ACCESS none; now commercial premises

Thomas Baldwin 1778

Thomas Baldwin 1778

Registry Office

Originally built as the Bath Savings Bank, this delightful little building was very up to date for its time, coming only four years after Charles Barry's Reform Club, which was in turn modelled on Sangallo's Palazzo Farnese in Rome. The architect of the Savings Bank, George Alexander, was a Londoner, and would undoubtedly have been aware of Barry's work. It is possible that the bank was the first in Britain to be modelled on an Italian palazzo.

The building is remarkable for Bath because it is isolated – not an element within a linear terrace. It is a perfect, symmetrical palazzo in miniature, with three bays on both of the principal façades. There are quoins at the angles, and a *piano nobile* complete with alternating segmental and triangular pediments – a motif that Barry himself did not adopt until later.

The building now serves as the Registry Office. The porch on the front elevation is a later addition.

LOCATION on the north side of Charlotte Street, by the car park entrance

George Alexander 1841

George Alexander 1841

Former Moravian Church

The Moravians were a protestant group that originated in Germany. In the mid-eighteenth century they built a number of utopian settlements in Britain – at Fulneck near Pudsey in Yorkshire, for example.

When compared with other Moravian settlements, this chapel has none of their architectural reticence. It is a fine, and very bold, neo-Roman composition (at a time in Bath's neoclassical period when the city's architects rarely turned to Rome). James Wilson seems to have been equally at home in the gothic idiom – his St Stephen's Church in Lansdown was built at the same time (see page 190).

The chapel's strong portico has a boldly modelled pediment supported by Corinthian columns with well-studied Roman capitals. It is placed in the centre of a two-storey main block, whose quoins defer to its neighbour, the Savings Bank (page 30), completed four years earlier.

LOCATION adjacent to the Registry Office in Charlotte Street
ACCESS none; the church is now a business bureau

James Wilson 1845

James Wilson 1845

Elim Chapel (The Percy Chapel)

H E Goodridge was the epitome of nineteenth-century eclecticism, having given Bath the fine Greek pavilions at Cleveland Bridge (1827, page 214); Beckford's Tower (1827, page 196); and a number of picturesque villas on Bathwick Hill, including Fiesole (1848, page 252), which is now the Youth Hostel.

The Percy Chapel was built for a breakaway congregation from the Argyle Chapel in Laura Place (page 228), for which Goodridge himself had provided a new frontage in 1821 in the Greek Revival style.

Here at Charlotte Street things were intentionally much different. It was not admired by the postwar purist Pevsner, who noted its 'awful, spreading Italian Romanesque façade'. Even today it is still difficult to appreciate fully this rich building, standing as it does with its ground-floor blind arcade right up against the pavement, facing north on a busy urban thoroughfare.

Internally, the galleried, polygonal major space (with the altar facing west) has a drab false ceiling at gallery level 'for reasons of economy'. There is a picture just inside the door of what it used to be like. The hidden part is especially worth seeing.

LOCATION on the south side of Charlotte Street, directly opposite the Registry Office

H E and A S Goodridge 1854

City Centre, North-west

H E and A S Goodridge 1854

Gay Street

This was originally a terrace of houses that continued the east side of Queen Square, but by the 1750s it had become a street with developments on both sides.

The highlight is no. 41, which faces Queen Square. Built in 1740, this was Wood's own house, with a playfully rounded window bay enclosing its diagonally-planned principal room. The building is now occupied by insurance brokers; its baroque style of architecture – through association with nineteenth-century commercial developments – suits its new function well.

The rest of the street is difficult to appreciate because of the enormous intrusion of the traffic intersection with its green signs, and the shop front extensions on the lower east side. Each house on the west side has three bays, and no. 8, 'The Carved House', was originally built by the sculptor Prince Hoare. Each house steps with the slope. Note the blind façade onto Queen Square Place, with its three pilasters framing 12 blind windows and a crude pediment above. This was built by the master mason John Ford, who did much work for the Woods.

LOCATION Gay Street runs northwards from the north-east corner of Queen Square

1750s

1750s

The Circus

Following the completion of Queen Square (page 22), Gay Street (page 36) was built northwards from it to connect with Wood's projected 'Grand Circus for the Exhibition of Sports'. It was, as Pevsner noted, the earliest Circus in Britain, and – according to Sir John Summerson – rather like the Colosseum of Rome turned inside out. This is because the architecture of both projects brings together three of the classical orders, one on top of the other – the Tuscan order at the bottom, the Ionic in the middle, and the Corinthian order at the top. But here at Bath they are used to form a round enclosure rather than a building.

The Circus is very tight; almost too tight. The internal diameter of 97 metres is the same as the north–south dimension of Queen Square. There are three uniform ranges of house fronts, with connecting streets between them. The length of these segments is subtly different – 10, 11 or 12 houses long – so that it is impossible to see a vista through the buildings. In this way, the form of the Circus can be appreciated only from within itself: indeed, it has been suggested that the intricate array of ornamentation on the façades demonstrates Wood's intention that they should be seen close-to.

The elder Wood died in 1754, three months after laying the Circus' foundation stone, and the project was completed by his son. As was normal for a speculative development of this kind, the individual units were constructed by different builders. Their internal plans vary greatly – as a glance at the haphazard backs proves – but the external treatment of the Circus façade is strictly uniform. There are 108 columns on each of the Circus' three orders. On the ground floor, the frieze features crisply carved motifs representing arts, sciences and occupations, and at the top of each range are female masks and garlands.

A number of alterations were made in the nineteenth century, including

John Wood the Elder 1754

John Wood the Elder 1754

the enlargement of the windows, but the robustness of Wood's architecture with its tiers of paired columns has ensured that the Circus' quality remains intact.

The central area has also changed, but for the worse. Early watercolours show a dramatic, empty cobbled space with no major central feature. Today's arrangement, with its roadway and separate green area with huge plane trees, denies a proper appreciation of the space.

The Circus should be liberated from all but the most necessary road traffic. It is not just world-scale architecture, it is also a domestic environment for a number of households who live behind the grand façades.

LOCATION walk north along Gay Street until you reach the Circus, now a mix of private commercial and residential usage

John Wood the Elder 1754

John Wood the Elder 1754

New (Upper) Assembly Rooms

There had been two older Assembly Rooms in the city – next to Terrace Walk – but both were demolished long ago. The site of one of them, Simpson's, which used to house public conveniences, has recently been taken over by a nightclub.

With the expansion of the city to the north-west, by the mid-eighteenth century the need was felt for new social premises, and a site facing the north-west corner of Queen Square was considered. Sadly, this came to nothing, and John Wood the Younger designed the present structure on its very poorly chosen site, hidden behind the east side of the Circus. What a shame that in a city full of wonderful urban spaces, this major building fails to contribute to a significant site – or even relate to one.

Externally, the building is dignified and plain. The two major volumes, which stand side by side, describe the two internal spaces – the Ball Room to the north and the Tea Room to the south – both huge by Bath standards. They are connected by a lower structure that is entered from the west. The octagonal Card Room in the centre of the plan had another rectangular Card Room added to the east in 1777 by an unknown architect. The single-storey colonnades around the outside provided shelter for the carriage of sedan chairs.

There is some effective detailing, especially in the Alfred Street elevation, with its first-floor windows treated as 'tabernacles', but elsewhere there is much empty wall space which begs for more ordering. The domestic idiom has been stretched to its limit.

With a capacity for 1500 guests, the New Assembly Rooms were the hub of the city's social life. Although written in the 1830s, when Bath was in decline, Charles Dickens' *Pickwick Papers* paints a delightful portrait of the Assembly Rooms in full swing:

John Wood the Younger 1769–77

John Wood the Younger 1769–77

... the Master of Ceremonies, in strict discharge of the important duties of his all-important office, planted himself in the rooms to receive the company. Bath being full, the company and the sixpences for tea, poured in, in shoals. In the ball-room, the long card-room, the octagonal card-room, the staircases and the passages, the hum of many voices, and the sound of many feet, were perfectly bewildering. Dresses rustled, feathers waved, lights shone, and jewels sparkled ... In the tea-room, and hovering around the card-tables, were a vast number of queer old ladies and decrepid old gentlemen, discussing all the small talk and scandal of the day ... Lounging in the doors, and in remote corners, were various knots of silly young men, displaying various varieties of poppyism and stupidity ... And lastly, seated on some of the back benches, where they had already taken up some of their positions for the evening, were divers unmarried ladies past their grand climacteric, who, not dancing because there were no partners for them, and not playing cards lest they should be set down as irretrievably single, were in the favourable situation of being able to abuse everybody without reflecting on themselves.

By the 1920s the complex had degenerated and was being used as a cinema and a market, and in 1942 it was gutted in an air raid. It has since been restored faithfully, and the magnificent interior is now as Wood designed it. The Ball Room is the largest space, occupying the full depth of the building. High-level windows run round three of the sides, and the chandeliers are, happily, the originals. The Tea Room, somewhat shorter with natural light on only two sides, has at its end a delightful colonnade supporting a musicians' gallery.

The Assembly Rooms stand now as a public memorial to an old social

John Wood the Younger 1769–77

John Wood the Younger 1769–77

order, in contrast with the eighteenth-century terraces nearby which still hum with life.

These terraces were set out by the younger Wood in the early 1770s to align with the New Assembly Rooms – not with either the Circus or Lansdown Road. Most of the houses in these streets are typical of their period, with three storeys above a basement, and three-bay façades. The details of individual houses vary – notice the original doorway of no. 14 Alfred Street with its figure of King Alfred.

The vista up Russell Street is pleasingly terminated by a bay window in Rivers Street.

LOCATION the Assembly Rooms between Alfred Street and Bennett Street are just to the east of the Circus, and may be approached by Bennett Street
ACCESS open daily 10.00–17.00 (11.00–17.00 Sunday); admission is free, but there is a charge to enter the Museum of Costume which is housed within the complex

John Wood the Younger 1769–77

John Wood the Younger 1769–77

Belmont

This handsome row of houses, best appreciated at the end of the view down Bennett Street, steps with the slope of Lansdown Road. Externally, the dwellings are of the standard design of the time, with three storeys of units of three bays each. There is a pediment above each of the offset entrance doors and above the central window of the *piano nobile*, or first floor. Compare the design with that of the Paragon (page 74), which was built at the same time.

As is proper for a terrace on such a sharply sloping site, there is no attempt to form a central emphasis, and the builders of each of the individual units seem to have pleased themselves when it came to choosing on which side of the façade to place the entrances (and hence the internal staircase). Like in the Paragon, the principal rooms face the rear to take advantage of the views across the Avon valley.

A handsome porch has been added on to the side elevation of no. 1 Belmont. Its serpentine plan is reminiscent of Thomas Baldwin's Cross Bath (see page 102).

LOCATION Belmont can be seen at the end of Bennett Street, which runs along the north side of the Assembly Rooms

1768–73

1768–73

Brock Street

The elder Wood originally intended that the streets radiating from the Circus should be short, each terminated by a grand façade. But his son extended Brock Street to make it a link between the Circus and his masterpiece at the Royal Crescent. Although many of the units on Brock Street have been heavily altered, it is still as conceived – a downbeat connection between two great events. Just look at the way the crescent is revealed at its western end.

Behind Gay Street and Brock Street, a more private Gravel Walk was built linking Queen Square with the Royal Crescent, for the 'convenience of inhabitants', in 1771. From it can be seen the modified backs of the houses on the west side of the Circus – a sublime arrangement of bay windows, battlements and dizzy spiral staircases. Here too is the entrance to the 'Georgian Garden'. The original layout of this garden to no. 4 The Circus was uncovered in recent excavations, and it has now been returned to its 1770 form. Because it was designed to be viewed from the house, there was no lawn area. The excavation was not able to establish the original species grown in the garden; it has been planted up following advice from the Garden History Society.

LOCATION Gravel Walk can be reached from Queen's Parade Place or Gay Street, or by walking downhill at the west end of Brock Street. The entrance to Royal Victoria Park (page 290) is close to the southern end of the Gravel Walk
ACCESS the Georgian Garden is open in summer (admission free); the entrance is well signed

1763–67

Brock Street 51

1763–67

The Royal Crescent

This crescent of houses forms one of the most spectacular urban spaces in Britain; it is also the culmination of the sequence of spaces, starting with Queen Square, conceived by the two Woods. This sequence – a kind of domestic version of a triumphal route – should be seen in the order in which it was built. From the north-east corner of Queen Square, the constraint of Gay Street leads to The Circus, in which tight hub the visitor turns left for the squeeze through Brock Street. And then – bang! – to the left, the view across the city towards the hills to the south, and to the right, the magnificent wall of houses.

The site for the new development was well outside the old city's boundary and was meadow and pasture land. It was acquired by the younger Wood in 1766.

The form chosen for this, the first of the city's great crescents, was very sophisticated. The curvature of the elliptical geometry was increased towards each end of the crescent so that the façades of the two end houses face each other. These façades were then continued round each corner to form handsome endpieces.

Overall, the architectural treatment is almost uniform. On a rusticated base stands a giant order of 114 Ionic columns. These support an entablature, with a balustrade hiding the garret windows. The rhythm of the columns is interrupted only at the centre, where they are paired either side of a round-headed window. This weak central accent has been criticised many times, and it is the one flaw in Wood's masterpiece. Otherwise the unique geometry works very well.

The intended uniformity of the composition is still convincing, despite some tinkering with second-floor sill levels and the absence in places of the original glazing bars.

A view of the rear reveals the development's piecemeal construction,

John Wood the Younger 1767–75

John Wood the Younger 1767–75

but there is strict uniformity on the façade. Wood's subleases to the individual builders were very carefully worded, requiring each one to erect his house 'in an uniform line with the whole pile of building'. It was also to be 'of the same height and with the like ornaments in front only' as the first house to be completed (at the east end, in 1769), which served as a model for the rest.

This same house, no. 1, has been fully restored and is now open to the public as an example of a Georgian town house.

Fortunately, the open space in front, reaching right down to Victoria Park, has remained undeveloped, and the Royal Crescent has been used as a dramatic backdrop to some spectacular concerts, firework displays and hot-air balloon launches.

City Centre, North-west

LOCATION best approached along Brock Street
ACCESS the 'Georgian House' at no. 1 is open
Tuesday to Sunday, and on Bank Holiday
Mondays; entrance charge (£3.50 for adults)

John Wood the Younger 1767–75

John Wood the Younger 1767–75

Marlborough Buildings

This fine terrace which runs downhill past the west end of the Royal Crescent was built on to the eastern edge of the common land that is now Victoria Park, and it marks the western edge of urban Bath.

Given the location, its principal rooms face westwards towards the open land. This means that the stairs are on the street elevation, and this has in turn given rise to the many later additions to the fronts.

Nos. 13–15, though not central, are more decorated, for they mark the end of the vista from Brock Street and across the front of the Royal Crescent. The design of these two houses, with their central first-floor windows, pediments set in shallow arches and decorative panels, is the main reason for the attribution to Baldwin.

Of the nineteenth-century excrescences, note the French Renaissance mansard roof crowning no. 25, which rises full height. The first-floor windows have iron shafts.

A walk uphill gives a good view back to the rear of the Royal Crescent and leads to St James's Square (page 170).

LOCATION at the west end of the Royal Crescent. From St James's Square, the tour could be continued to take in Cavendish Place (page 172), Cavendish Crescent (page 176), Somerset Place (page 184) and Lansdown Crescent (page 186)

attributed to Thomas Baldwin c. 1789

City Centre, North-west

attributed to Thomas Baldwin c. 1789

City Centre, North-east

St Michael's Church

The church stands on a very conspicuous – and difficult – site which closes the vista up Northgate Street, where Walcot Street and Broad Street join at a narrow angle.

The previous church here was certainly very handsome. It had been designed by John Harvey in 1742 in a Gibbs-like style, and presented an attractive slender portico towards Northgate Street. But being considerably smaller, it was demolished to make way for the present building.

Manners' gothic structure terminates the vista with a tall tower, which is pierced at the lowest level by three tall, narrow lancet windows. This tower, with its square base, octagonal lantern and tall spire, has caused consternation amongst critics – Pevsner called it 'crazy', and even Neil Jackson was hard-pressed to find precedents, having to go as far as Chartres or Freiburg to suggest something similar.

It is, nevertheless, a pleasing design. So too is the interior, where the tall aisles are almost the same height as the nave. There were galleries above the aisles until 1900.

LOCATION on Broad Street, start of the second central section walk
ACCESS the interior is open at most times

George Philip Manners 1835–37

George Philip Manners 1835–37

The Podium

The Hilton Hotel next door (1972, designed by Snailum, Le Fevre & Quick) did much at the time to destroy Bath's confidence in the modern movement in architecture. It was a crass response to such a challenging site. Just to its south, a podium was left vacant for new development, and this was earmarked for a new courthouse. Given the failure of its neighbour, here was an opportunity to do something really special. In the event, the courthouse was not built and a retail development was put on the site. It has been organised into two zones – to the south, nearest to Pulteney Bridge, a covered mall with small shops and cafés leads to the riverfront, while to the north there is a supermarket at ground-floor level, with the city's main library above, both with access from the mall.

This principal semi-public space has been shopfitted well, with pseudo-classical motifs of columns with four balls as capitals, and shallow arches. It has been done with a degree of conviction, but what a shame that the glazed roof, with its mandatory smoke vents and simplistic tubing, is so crude by comparison. Architecture and interior design still seem to be poles apart.

The outside of The Podium has caused controversy. The city's Georgian Group tried hard to get something better, but what has resulted can hardly be called studied. How bare it will all look in 30 years' time.

LOCATION on Northgate Street, close to the west end of Pulteney Bridge
ACCESS the mall is open during shopping hours

Atkins Sheppard Fidler 1989

Atkins Sheppard Fidler 1989

Broad Street

Now hopelessly dominated by through traffic, this street was one of the first developments outside the old city walls, and was completed before the age of the Woods. Although only three buildings survive from this period, they are important representatives of the 'transitional' phase of architecture in Bath, when builders started to use Palladian forms in preference to the medieval. Although it is difficult, and even dangerous, try to see these three buildings together from the other side of the road.

The Saracen's Head pub is right against the walls of St Michael's Church. It has two gables and a date of 1713. No. 41, of 1720, clearly an early try at Palladian architecture, has lost its attic storey, which probably had two gables. No. 38, of 1709, now belongs, like its neighbour, to a showroom (both have lost their original ground floors). It is another gabled building, in which the windows of the intermediate floors are set asymmetrically on the façade.

Other houses of this period can be found on both sides of nearby Green Street (just opposite St Michael's Church, which is worth a quick visit). Look for no. 14 on the left and the upper part of no. 3 on the right.

Shires Yard is entered through a gap on the west side of Broad Street. In this modern retail development by Bristol Team Practice, a public walkway threads beneath a glazed canopy on a tortuous route between gutted old buildings, with a difficult change of level as it reaches the other entrance on Milsom Street.

Further north on Broad Street, King Edward's School (Thomas Jelly, 1752) now stands unused. Of two storeys, with a handsome central pediment, it is a very competent piece of Palladian design.

LOCATION Broad Street runs north from St Michael's Church; Milsom Street can be approached through Shires Yard

Milsom Street

Now a busy shopping street, it was intended to be an extension of Wood's Queen Square development. In Egan's *Walks Through Bath* of 1819, Milsom Street was portrayed as 'the very magnet of Bath, and if there is any company or movement in the city, Milsom Street is the pulse of it'.

Its original architecture is similar to Bladud's Buildings (page 72), but here the units step with the gently sloping ground. The west side is almost completely taken up by shop frontages (Jolly's of 1879, in the centre of the street, is jolly and extravagant). But above ground floor there is uniformity throughout – each unit's central window is covered by a pediment, as was the standard of the time. The uniformity of the east side is interrupted by Somersetshire Buildings (page 68).

On both corners at the top end of the street are two typically Victorian bank chambers: on the east of 1865, and on the west of 1875, both by William John Willcox.

What a shame, though, that the vista up Milsom Street terminates so weakly in the three-bay pediment of the Edgar Buildings. This was a separate development, but contemporary with Milsom Street. Both were erected under Corporation leases.

LOCATION Milsom Street is the main north–south route in Bath, from the General Hospital to George Street

started 1762

started 1762

Somersetshire Buildings

Thomas Baldwin, architect of these buildings, belonged to the generation after the Woods, and worked for a while under Thomas Atwood. He was mainly responsible for developing the austere Bath Palladianism of these masters into a freer, more exuberant style, and designed some of the most significant buildings in the present city.

Somersetshire Buildings, a good example of his progressive approach, was originally five independent houses. Each end unit has a large pediment standing on fluted Corinthian columns; and the central unit bows outwards, with another giant order of Corinthian columns. All this stands on a rusticated base.

Walter Ison has suggested that Baldwin allowed himself this radical departure from the standard design because of his position as City Architect. In any case, it can hardly be called successful. The devices at the ends and the central bow are crammed up against each other and are far too bold for such a narrow space as Milsom Street, the architecture of which it disdains. But, in turn, Somersetshire Buildings have been intruded upon by the red terracotta and marble façade of the building society at the south end of the street.

LOCATION on the east side of Milsom Street, nos. 37–42
ACCESS none; now private commercial premises

Thomas Baldwin 1782

Thomas Baldwin 1782

The Octagon

Going to church was more often than not an unpleasant experience for the genteel folk of Bath. Not only were they cold, but they had to endure the bad odours that often wafted up from the crypt (certainly the case at Bath Abbey). To counteract these problems, the idea of charging a fee for a private seat in a private church was developed. The Octagon was erected as a commercial speculation to provide a comfortable place to worship. For a guinea (£1.05) a quarter, a room-like 'parlour pew' could be rented, with space inside for servants and the family. Good preachers were regularly brought in to pack the place out.

The central space was an octagon in plan, about 15 metres in diameter, with a continuous gallery above. There were two fires for warmth, generous windows – and no crypt with rotting bodies below.

From 1900 to 1935 the Octagon was an antiques showroom, but it is now home to the collections of the Royal Photographic Society. The fine interior is well preserved, but the original windows have been temporarily covered.

LOCATION on the east side of Milsom Street
ACCESS The Royal Photographic Society galleries, shop and restaurant are open every day except Christmas Day and Boxing Day, 9.30–17.30

Thomas Lightoler 1767

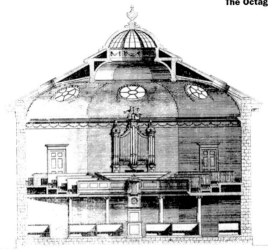

City Centre, North-east

Thomas Lightoler 1767

Bladud's Buildings

This comparatively early parade was the first of three great domestic developments along the east side of London Road. Its restrained Palladian composition, with central and end emphasis and a pedimented central window at the first floor of each unit, is now compromised by the semi-circular bay added to no. 6, and the shopfronts to the southern units. Try to imagine it without them. Occupying a prominent position on a steep slope, Bladud's Buildings, like the adjoining Paragon, have a superb aspect to the rear.

But unlike the Paragon, and unique in Bath, Bladud's Buildings' rear face is also given an architectural treatment, which can be seen from Walcot Street below.

Incidentally, Bladud was the legendary prince whose leprosy was cured by the local waters; he is supposed to have gone on and founded the city.

City Centre, North-east

LOCATION proceed to the top of Milsom Street and turn right along George Street; Bladud's Buildings are on the opposite side of London Road

Thomas Atwood or Thomas Jelly 1755

Thomas Atwood or Thomas Jelly 1755

The Paragon

The Paragon is the central of the three London Road terraces, with Bladud's Buildings to the south, and Axford's Buildings to the north. This continuous terrace, some 350 metres long, makes the east side of London Road one of the most satisfying groupings in the city. The Paragon curves gently with the line of the ancient road and – appropriately for a composition facing such a narrow enclosure – makes no grand gestures (except for the subtle articulation of each end). It reads as a uniform, linear piece – and very successfully so.

Its use of the standard elevational treatment required of all developments on Corporation land at the time also works, and if, as Walter Ison suggests, there was originally a balustrade along the top, it would have worked even better. Being further from the city centre than Bladud's Buildings, it has escaped being equipped with miscellaneous shopfronts and is more or less as originally built. The slightly raised pavement works wonders in separating the housing from the main road.

No. 20, on the opposite side of the road and set back behind its high hedge, is also by Atwood, c. 1770. Nearby is the popular Star public house, whose traditional interior is well worth a visit.

LOCATION a continuation of Bladud's Buildings, on the Roman road heading north out of old Bath

Thomas Atwood 1769–71

Thomas Atwood 1769–71

The Building of Bath Museum (formerly Lady Huntingdon's Chapel)

The Countess of Huntingdon's Connexion established churches in fashionable spa towns to appeal to a high class of worshipper. When John Wesley preached here in 1766, Horace Walpole (the architect of Strawberry Hill, Twickenham) was in the congregation. Although he admired the 'true Gothic windows', he found the building, with its balconies for 'elect ladies', too sumptuous.

The chapel itself cannot be seen from the road, and the 'exceedingly pretty little villa façade' (Pevsner) in Strawberry Hill Gothic to the front belongs to the house where Lady Huntingdon accommodated visiting preachers.

From 1932 the chapel became a Presbyterian church, and the 'little villa' the manse. In 1991 work was started to convert the lot into a museum explaining the history of Bath's Georgian buildings. The conversion is sensitive to the old building and forms a flexible forum for meetings and lectures, as well as the storage and display of information. It is a mine of information about Bath's architecture and should be the first port of call for any seriously interested visitor to the city.

LOCATION Vineyards, opposite the Paragon
RENOVATION Aaron Evans Associates
MUSEUM Michael Brawne & Associates 1992
ACCESS open Tuesday to Sunday, mid-February to end November, plus Bank Holiday Mondays; entrance charge (telephone 01225 333895)

1765

1765

St Swithin's Church

John Palmer also built Lansdown Crescent (page 186) and later went on to become City Architect. This church closely resembles Palmer's slightly earlier St James, Stall Street (which was badly bombed, and finally demolished in 1957), and is of a standard design of the time.

St Swithin's stands, dutifully facing east, at the point where Walcot Street runs off from the old London turnpike. Its delightful tower, with spire, rises from a base of ancillary rooms, while the major space is a two-storey box surrounded by a giant order of finely carved Ionic pilasters.

The central space of the interior is separated from each side by three Ionic columns, behind which runs a separate gallery. In the east wall, two plain glass windows above the galleries allow glimpses of the hills in the distance. The altar is in a small bay with a stained-glass window, projecting out above Walcot Street.

City Centre, North-east

LOCATION on Walcot Street, at the north end of the Paragon/Axford's Buildings

ACCESS open for worship only

John Palmer with Thomas Jelly 1777–90

John Palmer with Thomas Jelly 1777–90

Wood the Elder, in his typical way, said of Walcot Street: 'Instead of finding it covered with Habitations for the chief Citizens; it is filled, for the most part, with Hovels for the Refuse of the People.' Charles Robertson, in 1975, wrote that it is 'still a sad medley and no credit to Bath'.

This is not fair: there is real life in Walcot Street, with its colourful assortment of neighbourhood shops, an array of architecture that would do most town centres proud, a stone-masons' yard, an architectural salvage emporium, and two of the best public houses in the city. The area may have been blighted by the threat of being bulldozed for one of the over-ambitious road schemes of the 1960s, but that threat has probably contributed to today's vital hum.

Walking northwards out of Bath, the left side of the street is dominated by the backs of the houses to the west. Bladud's Buildings (page 72) have ornamented rear façades; those of the Paragon (page 74) have not. Arches built into the fall of the land make useful space for businesses.

Opposite, the long Corn Market, running perpendicular towards the river, is an early nineteenth-century listed building which was originally part of a larger market complex. In the 1970s it was in the path of a proposed 'Walcot Loop' road but, fortunately, it has been saved.

Further north, St Michael's Church House, designed by Wallace Gill in 1904, has a beautifully carved frieze and a delicate little spire. It should be pondered: here is a rare taste (for Bath) of the happy exuberance that the early twentieth century was capable of. It is now business premises.

Opposite, the remarkable little drinking fountain is not a medieval relic – it was put there in 1860 by C E Davis.

Walcot Reclamation, further up on the east side, has a constantly changing stock of architectural salvage. The new block adjacent to the

river is by Rock Townsend, and well worth a visit during opening hours.

Ladymead House, with its round windows facing the east side of the main street, has its entrance off a tiny court. It may well be the oldest surviving house in Bath – a painting in the art gallery on Bridge Street (by Pulteney Bridge) depicts it as a medieval building with many similarities to the present structure. Now housing, it was refurbished by MWT Architects and reopened in 1984.

Nos. 114 and 116 have a unique concave single-storey shopfront of 1823. Now an upmarket furniture showroom, this façade formed, until recently, the entrances to two dwellings. It was photographed, complete with net curtains, in Adam Fergusson's *Sack of Bath*. He wrote: 'The extraordinary shop front is just one of the many minor treasures which disappear from Bath year after year.' What a sad loss it would have been.

Chatham Row of 1767 is a plain row of two-bay Palladian terraced houses stepping down to the river. The end house, no. 12, with its charming Venetian window, was used by the city's Fire Department in 1967 to test the fire-resisting qualities of Georgian architecture. Though gutted by this exercise, it withstood the flames better than expected. It has now been completely refurbished. Nearby a flight of steps leads down to the secluded riverside.

The neo-Romanesque Walcot Village Hall, set back from the road and opposite St Swithin's Church, was built as St Swithin's Cemetery Chapel by James Wilson in 1842. The cemetery was closed in 1875. The green area nearby was used until recently for the annual Walcot Festival.

LOCATION Walcot Street runs parallel to Broad Street and The Paragon; Walcot Chapel (page 208) and Cleveland Bridge (page 214) are 200 metres to the north, after Walcot Street rejoins the London Road

City Centre, South-west

Royal Mineral Water Hospital (General Hospital)

The General Hospital was founded in 1716 'for the deserving poor', but the following years were spent pondering over where it should be, who would fund it and what form it would take. One idea was to have a circular-plan hospital with a bath in the centre, but since this form does not easily allow for future extension, the proposal was abandoned in favour of a linear plan.

The site of an old theatre close by the Borough Walls was eventually chosen, but the foundation stone was not laid until 1738. Wood was very proud of his building, which was originally two storeys high and in plan had two ward wings – one for men and one for women – running back from the Upper Borough Walls frontage. There were seven wards in all, with 108 bed spaces, and the possibility of extension southwards.

But in 1793, when expansion did become necessary, an attic storey by John Palmer was placed on top of Wood's two-storey building.

The main façade of the later extension to the west (Manners & Gill, 1850–60) is, for its time, very self-effacing. (Note their contemporary work on the old United Hospital by Pinch on Beau Street, page 108, which deserves comparison.)

LOCATION at the junction of Upper Borough Walls and Union Street; start of the third central section walk
ACCESS still in use as a hospital

John Wood the Elder 1738

John Wood the Elder 1738

Trim Street

Development of Trim Street started at the beginning of the eighteenth century and was amongst the first outside the old city walls.

Until 1969, many buildings from this period still remained, but then the western end of the north side was demolished to make way for the modern and depressingly banal Trimbridge House (John Bull & Associates, 1970). This was only one of the many unnecessary acts of vandalism committed against Georgian Bath during this time.

Further east is St John's Gate, or Trim Bridge, of about 1728. It leads to Queen Street and was cut through as part of Wood's Queen Square development.

Next door, no. 5, or 'General Wolfe's House', was built about 1720. Its five bays, with strongly emphasised horizontals, represent an interpretation of Palladian architecture that was fashionable just before Queen Square was built. A grander but otherwise very similar building was pulled down in the 1960s to make way for what is now Littlewoods' store.

Back at the west end, the Trim Street Presbyterian Chapel is now part of the nightlife of Sawclose. Built in 1795 by John Palmer, it has a rusticated ground floor and a tall arcade of windows. The little apse facing Trim Street was added in 1860.

LOCATION parallel with Borough Walls, 25 metres to the north

Beauford (or Beaufort) Square

John Wood the Elder, who had no time for Strahan, said of Beauford Square that it was 'partly a street, and partly a little open Area'. The same could be said today, since the square is still not sure which it is. At least Wood acknowledged that the houses of Beauford Square were of uniform character, unlike those in Strahan's other developments – Kingsmead Square (page 98), for example.

The south side is dominated by Dance's frontage for the Theatre Royal (page 92), with its metal-clad fly-tower throwing long shadows over the underused green space in front. The theatre entrance was originally on this side and would have brought some life to the place, but it is now a residential area.

On the east and west sides of the square are handsome matching two-storey terraces, but these are all that remain of Strahan's original development of 24 houses.

In the 1960s, the 'Battle for Beauford Square' may have been won by the preservationists, but the area is still let down by the kerbs and the yellow parking lines.

LOCATION from Trim Street, walk west across Barton Street

John Strahan 1736

Theatre Royal

The present building dates from 1805, when George Dance the Younger was commissioned to replace an earlier inadequate structure. Dance, architect of London's Newgate Prison, provided a fine frontage along the side of the auditorium facing Beauford Square (page 90), with doors and windows in the ground-floor arcade.

This frontage survives, but now that it is no longer the entrance to the theatre it is disappointingly sterile, although the windows of the principal dressing rooms still enjoy the view over the square. The strongly emphasised central element is adorned with pilasters whose capitals are in the form of theatrical masks. The two recessed side elements are unornamented to the point of abstraction, reminding us of the links between Dance and his pupil Sir John Soane.

The theatre's interior was rebuilt by C J Phipps after a fire in 1863, and as part of this redesign the entrance was moved from Beauford Square to the more prominent Sawclose. A house which had been built in 1720 by Thomas Greenaway was requisitioned for the purpose. It had been Beau Nash's first Bath home, occupied by him from 1743 to 1761. In the nineteenth-century remodelling, a single-storey extension was added to its front to accommodate the new box office. This lovely piece of vulgarity gives badly needed life to Sawclose: the bulbous capitals and polished brass fittings suggest for a brief moment that this may be cosmopolitan Brighton as opposed to fastidious Bath. Although the alterations to the Theatre Royal may not appeal to scholars, they did give the city one of its few pieces of exuberant stucco decoration.

Inside, the theatre boasts a number of ancillary front-of-house rooms with coal fires, which create an effective period setting. The auditorium itself, which is still as Phipps rebuilt it, is a lovely and intimate space in which no one seems to mind that the view from some of the seats is quite

George Dance the Younger and others 1805

George Dance the Younger and others 1805

restricted. Likewise, the view from the stage is of an audience close enough to touch. For the actor, there is another dramatic vista overhead, up into the fly tower, whose metal-clad exterior so effectively cuts out the sunlight from Beauford Square.

The backstage accommodation is as much a warren as the front-of-house, with small corridors leading to suites of dressing rooms, many of which contain period features that can allow the cast to soak themselves in the warm atmosphere of this, one of the country's best-loved provincial theatres.

City Centre, South-west

LOCATION from Beauford Square return to Barton Street and turn right into Sawclose; the theatre entrance is on the west side
ACCESS best seen during a performance, but there are occasional tours

George Dance the Younger and others 1805

George Dance the Younger and others 1805

What this ragged place lacks in spatial quality it certainly makes up for in night life.

At the north end, on the opposite side to the Theatre Royal, is the Blue-coat School (G P Manners with J Elkington Gill, 1859–60) with its tall tower on the corner with Borough Walls. The Jacobethan style was very popular elsewhere in the nineteenth century, but it had little impact in central Bath – except for here, at the earlier Bath Spa station (page 158) and, of course, on one of the gables of the Empire Hotel (page 124).

Moving south, past the parked cars, there is some exuberant late nine-teenth-century decoration on the east side in the entrance to an old theatre which has a shallow arch over a two-storey recessed balcony. This was the Regency, then the Palace. It closed in 1965 and is now a bingo hall.

Further south, just out of Sawclose on the corner with Westgate Street, is an Irish-themed public house, the old County Wine Vaults, with generous Italianate decoration and corner entrance.

On the other side of the street is Aaron Evans Associates' Seven Dials scheme (1991). Its first-floor veranda balcony (like those on Cavendish Crescent, page 176, or Raby Place, page 244) and the colonnade running up Sawclose are happy additions to the city. Notice how AEA have reinter-preted Pinch the Elder's stepping motif in order to handle the change of level on the colonnade.

Despite this motley collection of buildings, Sawclose needs no further improvements – except, perhaps, to get rid of the parked cars on the east side and turn it all into a vibrant street market.

LOCATION at the west end of Borough Walls

City Centre, South-west

Kingsmead Square

Despite the lack of any architectural unity, this is a popular place. The flagged central area with its large tree is connected to a range of six Georgian houses on the south side. A facelift in 1996 installed light green street furniture. However, in 1958, Pevsner called this 'no more than a junction of streets'. This southern range of houses had a motley mix of shopfronts attached to it, but by 1972 it was derelict, without roofs. Like Strahan's other major development in Beauford Square, today's tranquil scene masks a turbulent recent past. The area could easily have been overrun by the sort of sub-modern architecture (Rosewell Court, 1960) that can be seen in Kingsmead Street to the west.

The west side of Kingsmead Square is dominated by Rosewell House, which inspired the elder Wood to call Strahan's architecture 'piratical'. Its shape and the basic rhythms are conventional enough, but the exuberant decor-ative treatment is unique in Bath – it has been likened to south German domestic architecture. Rosewell House is another piece in Bath's impressive collection of pre-Wood classical architecture.

Given the popularity of the place and the architecture of Rosewell House, this is now the most European part of the whole city. But it could still do with some improvement: it needs a satisfactory link with Westgate Street and Sawclose just across the road, and it 'leaks' terribly towards the south-west. Perhaps a small development could be placed in the little triangular space?

LOCATION 50 metres to the south of Sawclose

John Strahan 1736

John Strahan 1736

Chapel Court and Hospital of St John

How wonderful that such a peaceful place can be found so close to the traffic and the bustle of the nearby shops. It is entered properly from the west, but also through a small gate behind the Cross Bath to the east. Most of the buildings of Chapel Court were rebuilt for the Duke of Chandos by Wood – despite the Duke's complaints of poor workmanship and faulty WCs. It was Wood's first major project in Bath.

In the courtyard, the buildings on the north and east side are by Wood. To the north is Chapel Court House and to the east the Hospital, with a strong arcade on the ground floor and a way through to Bath Street. The doorway in the corner is new, but otherwise it remains as originally built. To the south, under the new shallow arch, is the entrance to the little chapel, St Michael Within, built by Killigrew in 1723.

The south side of the court carries the date 1969 – and is very sympathetic for the time. The architect was Alan Crozier-Cole. Attached to it is a thoroughly refurbished early eighteenth-century house with gables and large, tight-packed sash windows. Chandos Buildings, also by Wood, are on the west side of the court.

To the south of all this, and on the south side of Hetling Court, is the gabled Abbey Church House (formerly Hetling House), which was completely rebuilt following war damage.

LOCATION from Kingsmead Square, follow the line of the old city wall southwards along Westgate Buildings; St John's Hospital has a small entrance off the pavement on the east side
ACCESS the chapel is generally open, but the gateway to the east is open only during the day

City Centre, South-west

John Wood the Elder, William Killigrew and others 1727

Cross Bath

The first bath on this site was established by the Romans. The old medieval structure of the Cross Bath (there used to be a cross in the middle) was given a new pump room by Baldwin in 1784. A few years later he rebuilt it entirely to make a suitable termination to the view along Bath Street to the east.

Its form and decoration are remarkable indeed: the centrepiece with its tall chimney is built on a gentle baroque double curve, reminiscent of Borromini's S. Carlo alle Quattro Fontane in Rome of 1634–82. Its sensitivity makes an interesting contrast with Baldwin's almost contemporary Somersetshire Buildings (page 68) on Milsom Street.

The open-air bath itself occupies only a part of the building; the rest is the pump room. The asymmetrical arrangement of the interior is completely disguised by the urban need for a symmetrical exterior at the end of the axis along Bath Street.

The interior was decimated in a conversion by C E Davis, c. 1880, but the lovely building has now been restored. During opening hours, a small display shows the previous sorry condition of the bath. When closed, the interior can still be seen through an opening on the south side.

LOCATION at the end of Bath Street, immediately in front of the small gate leading from the east end of St John's Hospital
ACCESS open Friday, Saturday and Sunday; voluntary contribution requested

Thomas Baldwin 1790

Bath Street

The street was formed by Baldwin as part of the Bath Improvement Act of 1789. With its slender 21-bay Ionic colonnades that open out into semi-circles at both ends, Pevsner called it a 'perfect piece of design'. It was built to connect the main baths complex in Stall Street (page 134) with a number of other baths to the west, including the Cross Bath (page 102), which Baldwin was busy remodelling at the same time, and which he used to terminate the axis of his new street.

Colonnades were built to provide shelter for the sedan chairs which carried their sick occupants in comfort from one pool to the next. They also lent their name to an ill-fated shopping development in the north-east corner, on the site of the old White Hart Hotel that was demolished in 1869. The Colonnades (Rolfe Judd, 1988) now stands empty. As a modern shopping development, it was destined to fail because its entrances were in the wrong place in relation to the city's main streets. The interior is not worth mentioning, and the entrance facing the Cross Bath is simply feeble. A suggestion that the Baldwin façade be continued was ruled out at the time as pastiche, but in hindsight it would have been a far better solution.

A restoration of the Colonnades site looks imminent at the time of writing.

LOCATION Bath Street runs east from the Cross Bath to the main entrance of the Pump Room complex
ACCESS The Colonnades is closed; the rest of Bath Street is in retail and commercial use and not worth inspecting

Thomas Baldwin 1791

Hot Bath

This was the younger Wood's only public commission. It was sited near the Hetling Spring, whose waters issued at 48°C. The building over the street to the west still carries the just legible words 'Hetling Pump Room'.

Externally the Hot Bath has little of note, but internally it is a superb piece of planning. It is a square building – the central part of which is the octagonal bath, measuring 6 metres across – which was originally open to the sky. Entrances from the street were on each of the four corners of the building. Each entrance led to a pair of changing rooms, making eight in all. Each changing room then gave access to its own submerged staircase, or 'slip', that led to the pool. These slips also served as discreet private baths.

The portico on the building's west side originally had a drinking water pump for public use.

Behind the building stood Decimus Burton's Tepid Bath of 1829. The curved wall on the north side of the Hot Bath was originally part of a colonnade leading to it. The Tepid Bath was demolished in 1922 to make way for the new bathing pool (closed for the time being).

City Centre, South-west

LOCATION just to the south of the Cross Bath
ACCESS currently closed

John Wood the Younger 1778

John Wood the Younger 1778

Beau Street: Technical School

The large building on the south side of Beau Street is the Technical School (originally the United Hospital), opened in 1826. With its north-facing portico, the main front, by John Pinch the Elder, bears some similarity to Wood's General Hospital (page 86). The heavy-looking attic storey was added by Manners & Gill in 1860.

In Bilbury Lane, just to the north, the pretty, low buildings belong to St Catherine's Hospital which was, according to the inscription, 'founded by Edward VI for the relief of poor aged persons, 1552'. It was rebuilt by G P Manners in 1829 in a minimal (and therefore cheap) Tudor style.

On the other side of Beau Street, Bellotts Hospital, founded in 1609 and rebuilt in 1859, has pretty relieving arches over the windows. The building was designed by Cotterell and Spackman. Like the old convent in Pulteney Road (now part of the Magistrates Court, page 152), there is a slight hint here of the influence of William Butterfield and G E Street.

LOCATION Beau Street runs from the south side of the Hot Bath back to Stall Street
ACCESS none

John Pinch the Elder 1826

Kingsmead Neighbourhood Redevelopment Scheme

The area of Kingsmead, to the south-west of the walled city, has always been the poor relation to the developments within the walls. It bore the brunt of German air raids in the Second World War and, with its many empty sites, presents one of the biggest challenges to the city's planners.

The original development of Kingsmead Flats was a typical interwar estate comprising 96 units. The award-winning redevelopment refurbished all the accommodation and provided a new total of 150 dwellings over the entire site, combining two- and three-bedroom flats with accommodation for the elderly.

The old deck access ways at the upper levels were converted into private balconies, and the open staircases were enclosed and protected by security systems.

A new community building is situated in the central courtyard, which is extensively landscaped, and many of the ground-floor units now have their own gardens.

The scheme involved a high level of consultation with the tenants, and all those who wished to remain in the area were able to do so.

LOCATION Kingsmead Flats are 300 metres to the west of Southgate; best viewed from the riverfront
ACCESS the central space, though easily seen, is private and inaccessible

Feilden Clegg Design, refurbished 1992

City Centre, South-west

Feilden Clegg Design, refurbished 1992

Green Park

This terrace is all that remains of an ambitious urban scheme conceived in 1790. These surviving buildings were the western range of a pair of terraces that formed a triangular space called Green Park with Seymour Street at its northern apex.

Seymour Street's western side was the first to go, making way for Green Park Station in 1869. Then, following bomb damage in 1942, the eastern range of Green Park Buildings was demolished in the 1950s. All this has been replaced by very mediocre architecture.

Of what does survive, the northern part – built in the 1790s – is typically chaste. The part nearer the river is nineteenth century and of larger scale. The three central units form a centrepiece that Walter Ison likens to Marlborough Buildings (page 56).

If the opportunity ever arises, either through traffic redirection or the redevelopment of its east side, Green Park should once again be contained by impressive architecture.

LOCATION 200 metres to the west of Kingsmead Square; can also be seen from the riverside walk, which can be joined anywhere west of Churchill Bridge

Green Park Station

The frontage building and train shed of this remarkable station survive intact, even though the last train rolled out of it in 1966. It was built as Queen Square Station for the Midland Railway in 1869, for services to Bristol and the North, and from 1874 the legendary Somerset and Dorset line from Bournemouth also ran into it.

The façade to the railway offices was given a happily respectable Palladian style by J H Sanders (compare this to Brunel's vulgar Jacobethan style at Bath Spa Station, page 158), and the dignified train shed by J S Crossley was – St Pancras fashion – good engineering, although completely unrelated to Sanders' building in front of it.

After closure, the station lay derelict for years, until Sainsbury's erected a supermarket on the land where the tracks used to be and refurbished the old buildings. The old station offices now have a brasserie on the ground floor, with meeting rooms above, and Crossley's train shed is both a craft market and a car park.

City Centre, South-west

LOCATION the station is conspicuously placed at the end of James Street, near the northern apex of Green Park ACCESS the train shed is accessible at all times

J H Sanders and J S Crossley 1869

J H Sanders and J S Crossley 1869

Norfolk Crescent

Like the Green Park buildings, this scheme was on the south-western fringes of the old city, and can probably be attributed to John Palmer, although Neil Jackson suggests that the guiding hand was that of Pinch the Elder. But unlike those in Green Park, this was a four-storey terrace and a satisfactory architectural solution had to be found to overcome this problem (see also Northumberland Buildings, page 28). Here, the central pediment in particular does not engage effectively with the entablature beneath it, which is supported by a giant order of pilasters.

Construction started on a piecemeal basis in 1792, but by 1810 only nine of the proposed 19 houses had been completed. The northern portion was bombed in the Second World War and later rebuilt with a sympathetic façade by the Corporation – but a look at the rear of this housing shows what is really going on.

The watchman's hut (1793) in front of the northern end of the crescent is a delightful survivor.

The low terrace to the north of the open space is Nelson Place, c. 1800; the western end was not finished until after the war.

LOCATION 500 metres outside the old city walls; can be approached by a long trek along James Street past Green Park Station or, even better, by the riverside walk

City Centre, South-west

1792

1792

City Centre, South-east

Much acrimony surrounded the start of construction of the new Guildhall in the 1760s. The two protagonists – Thomas Warr Atwood and John Palmer – had both prepared designs. Atwood was favoured by the Corporation (hardly surprising since he held a number of influential posts within the city, including that of City Architect), but Palmer offered to do the job for nothing in exchange for certain favours. The matter was resolved with Atwood's death, whereupon his assistant Thomas Baldwin took over the job and revised the design, even though construction to Atwood's design had already started. Building began in earnest in 1776.

Baldwin's Guildhall, five window bays in width, forms the centrepiece of the present High Street frontage, but the dome and the flanking wings are nineteenth-century additions. Originally a low screen on either side of the main building led to the markets behind, but these have gone to make way for the wings. From the car park at the rear of the Guildhall, its fine eastern elevation can be seen.

The interior was organised with a kitchen in the basement, offices on the ground floor, and a grand stair leading to the principal storey with its Common Council Room and the magnificent Banqueting Room (or Ball Room). The latter is approximately of the same width and height as Bath's two other great interiors – in the Assembly Rooms (see page 42) – and its length is exactly between that of the other two. But it is by far the most graceful room, with much elaborate plasterwork in subtle shades of green, beautiful chandeliers and a steeply tiered bandstand on the west side.

John McKean Brydon's nineteenth-century additions are sympathetic to the Baldwin design. To the south are additional offices (1891); to the east the Technical School (1891) and, round the corner in Bridge Street, the Library and Art Gallery (1898). The building only ceased to be the

T Baldwin (Guildhall) 1776; J M Brydon (19th-century extensions)

T Baldwin (Guildhall) 1776; J M Brydon (19th-century extensions)

seat of local government for Bath in 1996, when Bath City Council was consumed by the new Bath and North-east Somerset Council. The Guildhall is now part of this administration.

Sharing the urban block with the Guildhall complex is a small building that used to be a police station (C E Davis, 1865); it faces Orange Grove, next door to the massive Empire Hotel (page 124). Behind the Guildhall is the market, with entrances facing the river and on the High Street. Its 12-sided, domed central space carries the date 1863.

In Boat Stall Lane, just behind the Guildhall, there is a small surviving fragment of the East Gate (or Lod Gate), part of the medieval city walls.

LOCATION the fourth central section walk starts at the Guildhall; its principal frontage is on the east side of the High Street, which runs north from the Abbey; Bridge Street is the western extension of Pulteney Bridge
ACCESS the Banqueting Room is open during office hours (no charge)

T Baldwin (Guildhall) 1776; J M Brydon (19th-century extensions)

City Centre, South-east

City Centre, South-east

T Baldwin (Guildhall) 1776; J M Brydon (19th-century extensions)

Empire Hotel

In his book *Walks Within the Walls*, the celebrated British modern architect Peter Smithson goes right past the Empire Hotel but disdains to notice it, preferring to look the other way, to the 'roaring river'. The building remains a subject of intensely held feelings. Due to its sheer bulk and showy decoration, it is probably the most hated structure in the contemporary city.

Built during an energetic period of hotel construction throughout the country by C E Davis while he was City Architect, its five storeys, with an additional two in the roof, dwarf all around it, and show little respect for the Guildhall (which was being extended, much more discreetly, at the same time) or the Abbey. It has been suggested that the decorative themes of the top two storeys – a castle, a Dutch gable and an English house – symbolised the three classes of customer using the hotel. The height of these features has recently been reduced, but the loss of another two storeys from the body of the building may also have been advisable.

It ceased to be a hotel in the Second World War and was requisitioned by the military. During the decades of government service that followed, all the windows were screened by faceless ministry net curtains, hardly helping the building's image within the city.

At last it has been renovated – by PRP Architects – and turned into 45 luxury retirement flats, with a roof garden, library and card room. The critics who had argued for the hotel's demolition must now accept that it is going to be around for a good long time to come.

LOCATION behind the Guildhall, facing the river; cannot be missed ACCESS café and restaurant on the ground floor; Parade Gardens are open to the public (small entrance charge)

C E Davis 1901

C E Davis 1901

The Corridor

This early shopping mall was built by the architect as a personal speculation, and used to be known as 'Goodridge's Corridor'. Its main front
is a well-composed Palladian piece with a recessed three-bay central
portion flanked by two single-bay pavilions, and a canopy signalling the
entrance. The central section of the tiny mall is two storeys high with a
glazed roof. There is no public access to the first-floor gallery.

The far end of The Corridor emerges in Union Passage, known as Cox
Lane in the Middle Ages and now part of a thriving network of small
shops. In modern Bath it is probably as close as one can get to the scale
and bustle of the medieval city.

Goodridge also built the Bazaar in Quiet Street (1824) as a similar
development. It is now a bank, but the Corridor, fortunately, remains as
it was conceived.

City Centre, South-east

LOCATION the entrance is immediately opposite the Guildhall
ACCESS open at all times

H E Goodridge 1825

H E Goodridge 1825

The Abbey

Nowadays it is not really an abbey, or a cathedral, but a very dignified parish church that is fully engaged with the urban grain of the city.

In 1088, shortly after he had become Bishop of Wells, John of Tours considered that place to be too small for him and transferred his seat to Bath Abbey, with its thriving monastic community. A year later he bought the whole city from the Crown for £60, but by the twelfth century the bishop's seat had returned to Wells. To this day, the bishop is known as 'of Bath and Wells'.

There was originally a Saxon church on the site, and then a much larger Norman structure begun by John of Tours, but little of this survives above ground today. It was considerably larger than the present church: the apses at its eastern end extended well into what is now Orange Grove, and the high altar was where the taxis now park.

The present structure was begun in 1499 to replace the Norman church which had by then fallen into decay. It was the brainchild of Bishop Oliver King, who had apparently heard the message 'Let an Olive establish the Crown, and let a King restore the Church' in a dream. His vision is commemorated in the carved ladders with ascending and descending angels on the church's west front.

Much of the layout of the new church was determined by the foundations of the old – the present east front stands on the foundations of the old western crossing piers; and the old layout determined the uniform-bay spacing of chancel, crossing and nave, and gave rise to the rectangular shape of today's tower in plan.

King's masons were Robert and William Vertue (who built Henry VII's Chapel at Westminster and St George's Chapel at Windsor). The masons promised stone vaults of which there would be 'none so goodly neither in England nor in France'. But construction was not completed at once.

City Centre, South-east

By 1529 a Reformation parliament had been established in England which passed a series of acts cutting off the English church from Rome. In 1539, the final year of the mass seizure of all the monasteries, the priory was surrendered to the Crown, and the buildings sold on to one Humphrey Colles. In 1560 its gutted carcass was given back to the citizens of Bath to be their parish church. Later in the century a timber roof was built over some of the shell, and some windows were glazed. The nave finally received a timber roof in the early seventeenth century.

There were two major restorations in the nineteenth century: by G P Manners, the City Architect who later built St Michael's Broad Street (page 60) in the 1830s, and by Sir Gilbert Scott in the 1860s and 70s. Manners controversially provided the pinnacles all around the exterior, while Scott (who had so defaced the Royal Crescent by building his huge, and mercifully bombed, St Andrews in 1870 just behind it) sympathetically provided the fan vaulting in the nave in a way that probably conformed to the original intentions.

The small cloister on the south side was by T G Jackson, 1925.

What we see today is a remarkable achievement. The uniformity of the late gothic architecture has been kept faithfully intact by all the subsequent works: the intrusive Renaissance fittings, including a massive organ which broke up the interior, have now gone. The glorious fan vaulting, finally completed just over a century ago, is the crowning achievement.

ACCESS open in the daytime
(voluntary contribution requested)

1499–

1499–

The west front of the Abbey, with its famous carved image of angels ascending the ladder to Heaven, frames the eastern side of this enclosure; the Pump Room and Roman Baths complex is to the south, and to the north is a surviving terrace that includes General Wade's House (1715), now the National Trust shop. It has a Palladian elevation that predates Wood's influence. The giant order of pilasters mastering the first and second floor is original, but the arcaded ground floor has been replaced by a shopfront. Neil Jackson suggests that the attic storey (third floor) is an early precedent for the use of four storeys in Bath's domestic architecture. The attic on the house to the right is clearly an unfortunate addition. The façade beneath, again of the early eighteenth century, has been attributed by Walter Ison to Thomas Greenaway.

During the season, the Abbey Church Yard acts as a gathering area for visitors to the Roman Baths. It is a also a favourite spot for just sitting and watching the buskers, or queuing to enter the Roman Baths Museum.

LOCATION the open space in front of the Abbey's west end

The Roman Baths

Three hot springs rise within the old city of Bath, all within 200 metres of each other. One is near the Hot Bath (page 106), another at nearby Cross Bath (page 102), and the biggest – the so-called 'Sacred Spring' – comes to the surface beside the present-day Pump Room. The water, assumed to have fallen as rain thousands of years ago on the Mendip Hills away to the south, rises from a depth of 3000 metres to issue at a rate of 13 litres a second and at a temperature of 46.5˚C.

In prehistoric and Roman times the Sacred Spring was incorporated into ritual activities, and substantial fragments of a Roman complex devoted to worship and bathing survive today.

To its west, underneath what is today Stall Street, was the small temple of Sulis Minerva. Its pediment incorporated the famous 'Gorgon's Head' carving, a most dramatic piece of Roman sculpture which is now on display in the museum.

To the south was the Roman Great Bath, which in the second century AD was given a masonry roof. The walls and roof collapsed, but interesting brick and tile fragments of the roof were uncovered and are today presented in the position in which they were found.

Following the rediscovery of the Great Bath in 1880, a new structure was built around it which, though without a roof, corresponds approximately to the dimensions of the Roman building.

Smaller baths with their associated ancillary rooms and hypocausts have also been uncovered; so too has the Main Drain which carries the water away from the baths to emerge in the River Avon just beneath Parade Gardens. They can now be seen in the Roman Baths Museum.

LOCATION the entrance is beside the west front of the Abbey
ACCESS open daily 9.00–18.00 (admission charge)

The Pump Room

The function of a pump room was to serve the waters for visitors to drink in the most commodious way. Wood the Elder, when describing the earlier Pump Room on the site, wrote 'The Conduit yields the Water at two Cocks; and it stands with a Ballustrade, at such a distance as is necessary for the Waiters to receive the Water in Glasses, and hand it to the Company as they advance to the Rails.'

If you stand at the end of Bath Street looking east, the tall building on the left is where the first Pump Room (John Harvey, 1706) used to be. Before it was rebuilt, two new extensions were added. To the north, the colonnade leading to the Abbey Church Yard was built in 1786 by Thomas Baldwin; and in 1788 a similar frontage was added to the south side of the central building, to Baldwin's design. This was the entrance to the New Private Baths, now to the King's and Queen's Baths.

Around 1790, Baldwin started his rebuilding of the Pump Room, in the centre. The west façade facing Stall Street is by him. However, he fell out of favour with the Corporation in 1792 and work was continued by John Palmer – both of their names had already been enmeshed in the controversy over the design of the Guildhall (page 120).

Turn around now and look at Bath Street (page 104), which Baldwin was developing at the same time. The same architectural themes are repeated there, and in the Cross Bath (page 102) at the end.

Back in Stall Street, the extension to the south (to your right) is recent, replacing a disastrous piece by C E Davis of Empire Hotel fame.

It is likely that the Great Pump Room was completed to Palmer's design. There is a major Corinthian portico on the north front, and the interior is accessible to anyone wanting tea. It is of approximately the same dimensions as the Banqueting Room in the Guildhall, but not as sumptuously decorated.

City Centre, South-east

Visitors can still buy a glass of warm spring water, and stand and drink it at the 'Rails', while catching a glimpse of the steaming spa through the window beyond. All that is possible is done – with waiting staff, and musicians – to create the atmosphere of the Georgian period for the modern tourist, for whose convenience the large gift shop is close at hand.

If the next stop on the itinerary is the Roman Baths Museum, it is entered through what used to be the Concert Room. This was added to the east of the Pump Room, nearer to the Abbey, by John McKean Brydon in 1897.

City Centre, South-east

LOCATION the entrance is beside the west front of the Abbey
ACCESS open for morning coffee, lunch and afternoon tea

1700s

1700s

Orange Grove Buildings and Terrace Walk

Originally of the early eighteenth century, the parade of shops called Orange Grove Buildings in front of the Abbey's east end stand partly on the foundations of the Norman abbey's chancel. The buildings were refaced in 1897 by C E Davis and brought together in a unified composition. He left untouched the party-wall positions, window rhythm and upper gables, but added the ground-floor shopfronts, the hoods over the upper windows, and the corner feature. This was one of the kinder works by Davis, who went on to give the city the Empire Hotel immediately afterwards.

Around the corner to the south is Terrace Walk. In the eighteenth century there were Assembly Houses on both sides of Terrace Walk. On the west side, on the site of the existing buildings, were Lindsey's (later Wiltshire's) Rooms. These were designed by Wood the Elder in 1728, and demolished in the early nineteenth century. On the east side, on the site of the present traffic island (called 'Bog Island' after the subterranean conveniences that used to be there), stood the Lower Assembly Rooms, which were finally demolished in 1933.

No. 1 Terrace Walk (the Huntsman public house) has the earliest surviving shopfront in the city.

LOCATION Orange Grove Buildings are in front of the Abbey's east end

Masonic Hall (Friends Meeting House)

Built in year 5819 of the Freemasons' calendar, and passing out of their use in the year conventionally known as 1842, the hall was designed by the architect of London's National Gallery. As a piece of severe neoclassicism, the scholarly three-bay Greek portico, though predated by the Doric House (page 178), is earlier than the tollhouses on Cleveland Bridge of 1827 (page 214) or the Moravian Church in Charlotte Street of 1845 (page 32), which also has a portico with a pediment supported by two columns and antae. Pevsner notes that the Masonic Hall proves Wilkins to be 'a severer Greek than any of the Bath architects'.

Inside, the Great Room measures 15 metres by 9 metres.

LOCATION the entrance is on York Street, off the southern end of Terrace Walk
ACCESS not generally open to the public; services on Sunday and Wednesday morning

William Wilkins 1817–19

William Wilkins 1817–19

North Parade Passage and Ralph Allen's Town House

Most visitors to the city flock to visit no. 3 North Parade Passage, Sally Lunn's House, which in its present form is seventeenth century, though said to have originated in the late fifteenth century.

But the real architectural interest in this area hides behind here – a superb Palladian façade by John Wood the Elder of 1727 which stands at the end of an alley to the rear of Sally Lunn's. It can be seen fleetingly by going down the private passage at the rear of the Huntsman pub at the east end or by taking the preferred, but frequently closed, public entrance off York Street.

The façade belongs to Ralph Allen's Town House. Allen made his money out of the local postal service, which he reorganised to his own benefit. The Palladian façade is on an extension that he built to the house he bought in North Parade Passage. Its sumptuous three-bay elevation has a giant Corinthian order supporting a richly modelled pediment. In the centre there is a large round-headed window with a 54-pane sash. Try to imagine this with nothing between it and the hills away to the east. This was the case when Allen built his Sham Castle in 1762 (page 262), positioned so that he could see it from this house.

City Centre, South-east

LOCATION the façade of Ralph Allen's Town House can be viewed from the alley – although this is frequently locked – beside the Friends Meeting House in York Street
ACCESS no access to the Town House, which is in commercial use

John Wood the Elder 1727

John Wood the Elder 1727

Abbey Green

Originally the site of the monks' bowling green, this was noted by Pevsner in 1958 to be 'an irregularly shaped forlorn little square with a big plane tree'. It is now, as Charles Robertson says 'a charming oasis'. Peter Smithson talks of sitting underneath the tree and feeling at the edge of the 'iron and stone technology'.

It is indeed a tranquil urban space, to which much life has been added by the popular and student-friendly Crystal Palace pub on the west side. St Michael's Arch in the south-west corner is a more recent addition – part of the Marks & Spencer development of 1973.

A short detour to the east, back along North Parade Passage, takes us to North Parade Buildings (originally Gallaway's Buildings). This short cul-de-sac of uniform three-storey Palladian houses of 1750 is attributed to Thomas Jelly. Beyond the railings at the south side used to stand John Lowder's extraordinary National School, built in 1816. It was a round building with wedge-shaped classrooms, accommodating 1000 pupils, but demolished in 1896.

LOCATION at the west end of North Parade Passage

North and South Parades; Pierrepont Street and Duke Street

As early as 1725, Wood had plans for this difficult, undrained site known as the Abbey Orchard. When he started work in 1740 he hoped to build a complete 'Royal Forum' – a vast square surrounded by houses that were easily as fine as those in Queen Square, and bisected by the River Avon, which was to be canalised. In the event, all that was built were the blocks on the north side of the Forum – defined by North Parade, South Parade, Pierrepont Street and Duke Street – and their execution in no way matches the grandeur of the conception.

North Parade was intended to form part of a 160-metre-long terrace facing what is now known as Parade Gardens. Wood raised his buildings by over 5 metres to overcome the drainage problem, and intended that the retaining walls be given a rusticated architectural treatment to harmonise with the houses above. However, the individual builders who had leased the plots from Wood thought otherwise and built the walls out of plain rubble.

To the west, the Pierrepont Street elevation, with its centrepiece Century House, is unkempt. St James's Portico opposite gives access to Pierrepont Place and Orchard Street.

To the east, Duke Street with its beautiful pavement is exceedingly handsome.

South Parade was to have been the northern side of the vast Forum. When looking at it today, a vast amount of imagination is needed to appreciate the scale of this unrealised project. Many of the buildings have been altered – and the gilt tiles of Pratt's Hotel, the emblems of various touring clubs, and the randomly altered *piano nobile* windows and insipid balcony railings do nothing at all to help.

In 1993 the Bristol architect John St Leger proposed the completion

John Wood the Elder 1740–48

John Wood the Elder 1740–48

of the Forum and the flooding of the great square with water from the river, leaving St John's Church (page 154) marooned in the centre on a picturesque island.

Before leaving the Parades, it is worth mentioning the two lodges at the east end of North Parade Bridge which are now rather dwarfed by the Sports Centre. They were built in 1836, at the same time as the bridge, by Edward Davis in the Jacobethan style. Look at the extravagantly moulded windows on the outer faces. Davis (father of C E Davis of Empire Hotel fame) had been a pupil of Sir John Soane; he also laid out Victoria Park.

The Magistrates Court (page 152) is just a short walk further east along North Parade Road, and worth the visit.

LOCATION North Parade forms the southern edge of Parade Gardens; North Parade Bridge is its easterly extension

John Wood the Elder 1740–48

John Wood the Elder 1740–48

Magistrates Court

This convincing new court building is adjacent to the old buildings of the Convent of La Sainte Union by J Elkington Gill, designer of the Bluecoat School next to Sawclose (page 96). The old convent now accommodates court functions.

The new building clearly borrows motifs from its neighbour, but establishes its own independent aesthetic, with very well-detailed external timber work, especially to the windows and eave soffits.

The Courthall on the first floor (accessible to the public) is the most dignified modern internal space in Bath. Its marble-clad walls with clerestory windows, and its uplit ceiling with exposed lines of structure are well worth seeing.

LOCATION 200 metres east of North Parade Bridge or, alternatively, 400 metres south of St Mary's Church (page 244) along Pulteney Road; entrance on North Parade Road.
Widcombe Primary School (page 268) and the Dolemeads Estate (page 270) are 300 metres south along Pulteney Road
ACCESS open Monday to Friday during working hours

Avon County Council (Chris Bocci) 1989

City Centre, South-east

Avon County Council (Chris Bocci) 1989

154

St John the Divine Roman Catholic Church

In general, nineteenth-century enthusiasts for gothic architecture felt contempt for the plainness of Georgian architecture, and to prove their contempt they built St Andrew's on Julian Road (Sir Gilbert Scott, 1870, now gone) and St John's here on Manvers Street. With its many-gabled bulk, rough-faced finish and 67-metre-high spire, it makes no attempt to integrate itself with the scale and grain established in the Parades. But, as Charles Robertson puts it: 'its neighbours to the west and south, the car park and the ... Police Station, are scarcely entitled to demand any apology.'

Inside, the spacious nave has a comparatively plain vault, but the chancel, with its delicate gilt iron screen, is richly decorated. Two colourful rose windows illuminate the transepts.

Following bomb damage in 1942, the south range was rebuilt as a new Presbytery by the Alec French Partnership. During roof repairs carried out in 1994, the original polychromatic slating scheme was reinstated.

The whole composition looks very dramatic when viewed from the other side of the river.

City Centre, South-east

LOCATION set back from Manvers Street; the entrance is on South Parade
ACCESS open during the daytime

C J and E J Hansom 1863

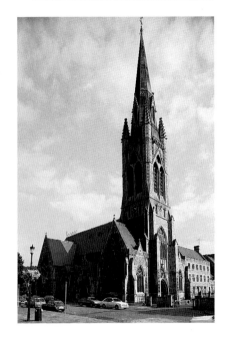

C J and E J Hansom 1863

Two Hotels, Manvers Street

Lord Manvers made precise directions in the Great Western Railways Act of 1835 about how Manvers Street should be established. It was thus one of the first railway approaches to be laid out according to legislation. However, the only part to be built of what could have been a very dignified piece of urban design was this pair of almost identical hotels immediately opposite Brunel's station. They both turn their corners convincingly with a giant Ionic order of columns. The eastern hotel – the Argyll – is now isolated on a busy corner of the bus station. The western hotel is in better shape and is in use as the Royal Hotel. It used to be connected with the station platform by a bridge at high level – you can still see where.

If only Brunel's station had been of similar quality – and the intended terraces of Manvers Street and Dorchester Street built – the composition might have been one of which Bath could be proud.

LOCATION Manvers Street is the north–south axis beside the Parades, with Bath Spa Station at its southern end

attributed to H E Goodridge c. 1840

City Centre, South-east

attributed to H E Goodridge c. 1840

Great engineering and architectural care was taken in navigating the railway into Bath. In Bathwick, a kilometre to the north, Brunel had to construct a massive retaining wall for the Kennet and Avon Canal (page 242). Despite some patchy brick repairs, this is still a beautiful stone structure, completely in sympathy with the grand Georgian terraces which Bristol-bound passengers can see through the carriage windows.

There are some graceful bridges over the line as it passes through Sydney Gardens, where the public park reaches up to the tracks, offering a classic view of the trains as they round the curve into the city. The track soon finds itself having to cross the river twice to accommodate Bath Spa Station, at the tip of the city's peninsula.

St James's Bridge, to the north-east of the station, is a handsome skewed structure with a 27-metre span. The riverside walk passes beneath it.

Bath Spa Station has a disappointing frontage by Brunel with paper-thin Jacobethan gables. It makes some attempt to terminate the vista down Manvers Street. As with many early GWR stations, there was originally a glazed canopy over the tracks, but this went in 1897.

Leaving the station towards Bristol, the line crosses the Avon again by a lattice girder bridge, then passes over two roads by a turreted, sham gothic viaduct.

I K Brunel: Bristol to Bath 1840, Chippenham to Bath 1841

I K Brunel: Bristol to Bath 1840, Chippenham to Bath 1841

Much has changed recently for the area of the city running south from Southgate. The Littlewoods and Marks & Spencer stores stand where John Palmer's St James's Church used to be. Both built in the early 1960s, they have been described, accurately, as 'Neo-sub-Georgian'. What used to be Horse Street ran nearby from the South Gate in the city walls down to the river at the Old Bath Bridge. Today the road, now called Southgate, has on its east side a 2-hectare shopping development of 1973 by Owen Luder. The *Architectural Review* at the time commented that it was totally out of keeping with Georgian Bath.

Controversy still surrounds the future of this site and the way in which the bus station behind it links with the city centre. Although the popularity of the pedestrianised street cannot be denied, the loss of Luder's Southgate shopping development should be no cause for concern. It is said to be imminent.

LOCATION at the southern end of the city's main shopping thoroughfare, 200 metres to the west of Bath Spa Station

North-west of Centre

Christ Church

Established as a free church where the city's poor could worship, Christ Church was the first large Gothic Revival building in Bath. Ten years earlier, Palmer had built All Saints' Chapel – a delightful piece of 'Gothick' wallpapering, now demolished – between Park Street and Lansdown Crescent, but here the idiom was used in a far more serious manner.

Nevertheless, Christ Church is still more or less a plain box with gothic trimmings and a tower with various anterooms at the west end. Anything finer would have been inappropriate and too expensive for such a humble congregation.

There was space on the ground floor for 800 non-fee-paying worshippers, with places up in the galleries let to help pay the costs. This interesting social division was reflected on the original exterior – small quatrefoil windows allowed light into the lower level, while the larger windows illuminated the galleries above.

The quatrefoils have now gone and the battlements have been replaced; an apse was added in 1886.

Just behind, and now part of the Bath Industrial Heritage Centre, is a real tennis court of 1777, with a display outlining the complexities of the game.

LOCATION on Julian Road, which runs west from Lansdown Road, 150 metres to the north of the Circus
ACCESS open for worship only

John Palmer 1798

John Palmer 1798

Portland Place

The area north of what is now Julian Road was built up at the end of the eighteenth century, but the only developments with an urban presence were St James's Square (page 170) and its contemporary, Portland Place.

This forms a triangle with the main terrace to the north, and it could well be the most unrecognised area in urban Bath, simply because it connects to nowhere – as when it was built.

Like Edgar Buildings in George Street, it is elevated on steps – here there are ramps for the rich disabled (two centuries before the Building Regulations required them for everybody) – and the architecture is plain to the extreme. The central part, with its pediment, is subtly designed with only the gentlest hint of depth – it stands just forward of two outer elements which are slightly splayed so that they in turn stand forward of the rest.

This main part is also notable for the way in which it makes a composition out of three tiers of windows of the same size by using only three string courses. This is the sort of architecture that should be studied by today's housing architects, who are often faced with the dilemma of having to provide identical accommodation on several floors while bringing the whole into an architectural unity.

To the east, the Ballance Street housing development was hated when it was built in the 1970s because it replaced some small-scale terraces typical of Bath in 1770. Adam Fergusson, in *The Sack of Bath,* was about right when he wrote that it could have been built 'anywhere from Brasilia to Bracknell New Town'.

LOCATION 100 metres to the north of Julian Road, along Burlington Street

attributed to John Eveleigh 1786

attributed to John Eveleigh 1786

St Andrew's School

This delightful little building sits well on its demanding site, immediately opposite the open space where Sir Gilbert Scott's huge, bombastic church of St Andrew used to stand until it was bombed.

The key generator of its form is the low rubble wall that runs around the back of the pavement line. Occasional windows let into the wall at low level relate to the teaching spaces inside – a child can sit in one of the round openings and watch the world go by.

The heavy masonry base contrasts with the colourful metal frame that sits upon it, supporting the roof.

There is, throughout, a playful but careful use of decorative elements, symbolically reflecting the building's role as a church school. The blue roof ventilators carry references to builders' set squares – and both internally and externally there is much carved stonework by James Leask.

The same practice completed Widcombe Primary School, with many similar design generators, in 1996 (page 268).

North-west of Centre

LOCATION at the west end of Julian Road; Widcombe Primary School is on Pulteney Road

Nealon Tanner Partnership 1991

Nealon Tanner Partnership 1991

St James's Square and Park Street

This rectangular open space, with diagonal streets running away from each corner, has much in common with Wood's Queen Square – the north and south elevations are dominant compared to the identical east and west elevations, which step down with the fall in ground towards the south. St James's Square is a more elongated rectangle with a longer north–south dimension.

Nowadays the trees are too large and there are too many parked cars, and there is not enough architecture on the longer east and west sides to do justice to this potentially great place – their central and end emphases with the ornamented *piano nobile* are either unnecessary or inadequate.

Through the five-bay unit on the east side an arch leads to St James's Place, a delightfully hidden city space. At the south end there is a glazed arcade containing – a launderette.

Park Street at the north-west corner is a quiet backwater – there is now too much variety in the height and the treatment of the units to get close to achieving the drama that might have been. At the north end of its vista stood, until bombed, Palmer's All Saints' Chapel, Lansdown (1794). Pinch the Elder, who built the upper houses around 1808, had intended to continue north-west towards Somerset Place with the unbuilt 'Regent Place' – you can see the angle of it on the last unit of Park Street.

LOCATION St James's Square is reached via St James's Street or Marlborough Street at the west end of Julian Road; Marlborough Buildings (page 56) and the Royal Crescent (page 52) are just to the south

John Palmer 1794

John Palmer 1794

Cavendish Place

It is best to approach Cavendish Place as originally intended, by leaving St James's Square by its north-west corner, on to Park Place. Now facing the golf course, Cavendish Place was started by Pinch in 1808. It steps majestically up the steep slope, with a scrolled string course jumping from unit to unit by means of Pinch's quadrant ramps. No. 3 occupies the corner with Park Place, and the whole transition from John Palmer's earlier development (page 170) has been handled well (although Neil Jackson disagrees, arguing that 'nos. 1, 2 and 3 Cavendish Place do not seem to belong to the terrace at all'). The houses still have their delicate iron-railed balconies, most of which would have originally had verandas.

Further up Cavendish Road is Winifred's Dale, a semi-detached pair of houses with bow windows that is attributed to Pinch, c.1810. Although clearly two separate houses, the architecture brings them together in a convincing way.

LOCATION can be approached via the north-west corner of St James's Square or directly from the south along Cavendish Road, a continuation of Marlborough Buildings

John Pinch the Elder 1808

John Pinch the Elder 1808

Cavendish Lodge

Sandwiched between Winifred's Dale and Cavendish Crescent, this new apartment building with its two 'lodge-style homes' flanking the entrance drive had a difficult passage through the planning process. It is all in a deeply committed classical idiom, which has – inevitably – provoked the wrath of architects preoccupied with the sterile modern/classical debate. Let us take it as a serious contribution to Bath's architectural portfolio.

The principal block is set back some way from Cavendish Road, roughly where the earlier Cavendish Lodge used to stand. The rusticated ground floor, which contains the main entrance hall, is set into the sloping ground, and above it stand three storeys of dwellings. The west elevation, which faces the road, is adorned with a flight of steps and a pediment. The main entrance, with another pediment and protruding wings, is on the south front. Great care has been taken to graft the classical language on to what is, of course, a modern building. But there are compromises, many of which were imposed on the architect. Especially worrying is the underuse of the site, with strangely isolated small garage blocks flanking the prolonged entrance drive.

The entrance lodges are, externally at least, a pretty touch. Their unpointed rubble walls are great fun.

North-west of Centre

LOCATION on Cavendish Road, between Winifred's Dale and Cavendish Crescent
ACCESS none

William Bertram and Fell 1996

William Bertram and Fell 1996

Cavendish Crescent

Cavendish Crescent, further north from Cavendish Place, was started in 1817 as part of a speculation by the builder William Broom, who went bankrupt in 1825. Here, and at the later Sion Hill Place (page 180), Pinch's architecture shows none of the exuberance of his earlier terraces (for example, Sydney Place, page 238). Cavendish Crescent is a more austere but nevertheless dignified piece. It is a uniform four-storey composition of identical three-bay units (except for the veranda on no. 9), brought together only by the horizontals of the first-floor band, the third-floor string course, and the entablature. The stepping up of each of the units is subtle, but not enough for Pinch to celebrate with his usual quadrant ramps. Neither the centre nor the ends are articulated, and the gable facing the road is completely bare. This is all the more surprising considering the architectural display that had just been built on the other side of the road at Doric House (page 178).

North-west of Centre

LOCATION at the top of Cavendish Road

John Pinch the Elder 1817–30

John Pinch the Elder 1817–30

Doric House

Reaction to the extraordinary exterior of this building high up on Sion Hill has ranged from 'forbidding' (Pevsner) to 'one of the most beautiful and original small works of the Greek Revival' (Walter Ison).

It was built for the Bath-based painter Thomas Barker as a small public picture gallery. The interior still contains a large fresco by Barker and has some gracious fittings. But it is the exterior, designed by Sir John Soane's protégé Joseph Michael Gandy, which is available for us to admire at all hours.

A previous scheme of 1803 proposed a single-storey elevation facing the road, of five bays standing on a massive plinth. The version built is divided into two storeys, each with a severe Doric order. This allows windows to be placed at a higher level, above the blank wall upon which the fresco was painted. The entablatures are continued round to the astylar south-facing garden elevation with its central windows.

For other examples of the Greek Revival in Bath, see William Wilkins' Masonic Hall (page 142) and H E Goodridge's Cleveland Bridge (page 214).

North-west of Centre

LOCATION at the top of Cavendish Road, opposite Cavendish Crescent

J M Gandy c.1805

J M Gandy c.1805

Sion Hill Place

This terrace hides behind dense planting at the northern fringe of the city. There are many design similarities here with Pinch's earlier terraces – at Sydney Place (page 238) and, more recently, at Cavendish Place (page 172) and Cavendish Crescent (page 176). They all have four storeys, although here many of the units are only two bays wide and, as the site is level, there is no stepping.

The terrace is very well composed, with Pinch's favoured round bows at either end and a played-down central emphasis, all forming a palace-type composition.

The original intention was to place first-floor verandas at either end and in the centre – again, these were a favoured Pinch motif (see Cavendish Crescent, and Raby Place, page 244).

The unit at the west end has been extended to house an art collection. It incorporates an eighteenth-century façade from a building in Chippenham High Street that was demolished to make way for a Woolworths store.

North-west of Centre

LOCATION Cavendish Road continues uphill as Winifred's Lane; turn left on Sion Road to Sion Hill Place

John Pinch the Elder 1818

John Pinch the Elder 1818

Kingswood School Nursery

Set inside kitchen-garden walls, and built against the sloping hillside, this small school is hidden from the public gaze. Its low elevation is made up of classrooms grouped on either side of a central entrance. Full-height glazed classroom doors allow for connection with the outside in summer.

The service accommodation is at the back of the linear form, which is articulated by double-height spaces accommodating reception, library, and computer areas. The major space containing the top-lit assembly hall and gymnasium is at the eastern end.

The building employs a high level of natural servicing. The principal spaces are naturally ventilated, and natural lighting is admitted into the centre of the plan by high-level glazing.

Materials, colours and scale make this scheme a completely appropriate response to its function and location. It won a regional RIBA award in 1996.

North-west of Centre

LOCATION in private grounds to the west of Sion Hill Place. Once through the gate one can see the Chippenham façade of Sion Hill Place
ACCESS none

Feilden Clegg Design 1995

Feilden Clegg Design 1995

Somerset Place

The interest here is undoubtedly in the central feature – a pair of dwellings united beneath a split segmental pediment that is unique in the city. The terrace continues the sinuous line established by Lansdown Crescent, which was started at the same time. However, construction of Somerset Place began not at its eastern end but with its two central houses, which have no curvature in plan and are at the high point in the ground. The units either side step down.

The development was stricken by the financial crisis of the 1790s and was not continued until about 1820. Of the western units, only the vaults were ever completed.

Much rebuilding has taken place following substantial war damage, especially at the west end. The terrace is now used by Bath College of Higher Education's art school, whose shop in one of the basements offers a very good selection of artists' materials.

LOCATION just uphill from Cavendish Crescent (page 176)
ACCESS the art shop is open weekday mornings during term time

North-west of Centre

John Eveleigh 1790

John Eveleigh 1790

Lansdown Crescent and Lansdown Place East and West

Standing high on the city's northern slopes, this is Bath's most prominent architectural set-piece.

Like Thomas Baldwin's Cross Bath (page 102) of a few years earlier, Lansdown Crescent also has a double curve on its façade, but on a much grander scale. The 20 units in the main part of the crescent form a third of a circle with a radius of some 100 metres. It makes an interesting comparison with the earlier Royal Crescent (see page 52). In Wood the Younger's piece, which is somewhat larger, the curvature varied, while here it is constant. And the architectural treatment of the Royal Crescent, with its giant order of engaged Ionic columns, is louder and ubiquitous. At Lansdown, much weaker pilasters are confined to the central part. It is a uniform and elegantly restrained three-storey design, rusticated throughout, with fine overthrow lampholders to each unit.

The design of the central feature has been criticised, but it does succeed in making an architectural composition out of the problem of having the exact centre on the line of a party wall. Note how John Eveleigh dealt with the same problem at the same time in Camden Crescent (page 202).

Here at Lansdown the two central houses have been brought forward subtly from the wall surface of the surrounding houses. A portico motif of four widely spaced giant-order pilasters supports a pediment and the central bay of the giant order is widened to admit an arched recess at first-floor level.

At either end of the central terrace are larger units with bow windows, forming good 'book-ends' to the composition. There are then breaks before the 'undulating wall' continues to either side with Lansdown Place East and West. In the 1820s a bridge was built over the western break by William Beckford, who owned the two houses on either side.

John Palmer 1792

John Palmer 1792

In the garden of no. 20 Beckford built his 'Islamic Pavilion', which marked the start of the picturesque walk up to his tower on Lansdown Hill (page 196).

The two flanking Places were badly damaged in the last war.

The crescent still looks out on to open land, with sheep grazing on the opposite side of the roadway, and there are magnificent views across to the hills to the south. Originally, Palmer's All Saints' Chapel stood on the slopes just below, where Chapel House is now.

LOCATION continue eastwards from Somerset Place; alternatively, if coming up Lansdown Hill, Lansdown Place East is on the left-hand side (if coming up from the city centre, you will have passed Camden Crescent, page 202, on the right – it is an exact contemporary of Lansdown Crescent, and deserves close comparison)

John Palmer 1792

North-west of Centre

North-west of Centre

John Palmer 1792

St Stephen's Church, Lansdown

Pevsner used the same word to describe the tower of this church and that of St Michael's Broad Street (page 60) – 'crazy'. It is true that the classically-trained Wilson could at times be undisciplined in his use of the gothic idiom, but this tower, with its pinnacles and traceried flying buttresses supporting the inner octagonal body, is surely rather attractive.

The local bishop refused to consecrate the church at the time because it was not orientated east–west (because of its site it was north–south). The transept was hastily added to make amends, but this led to financial problems, and consecration did not occur finally until 1880, when the chancel was built by William Willcox (who had entered partnership with Wilson in 1866).

The interior has a delightful painted timber roof. The rear portion was partitioned at low level in the 1960s to provide a meeting hall. The entire basement vault was remodelled in 1994 by Slade Smith & Winrow to extend the meeting facilities and create the St Stephen's Centre.

Just downhill from St Stephen's is a row of houses called St Stephen's Villas. These were built as almshouses for St Swithin's Church in Walcot (while it remained unconsecrated, St Stephen's acted as a Chapel of Ease to Walcot). The original proposal was much larger – there were to have been 16 houses, with a large chapel in the centre of the group. In the event, only six were built, designed by James Wilson in 1843.

LOCATION St Stephen's is the conspicuous church high on Lansdown Road, 200 metres north of Lansdown Place East; St Stephen's Villas are 100 metres south of the church, on St Stephen's Road

James Wilson 1840–45

James Wilson 1840–45

The Royal School

The school, originally the Lansdown Proprietary College and then, following bankruptcy in 1865, the Royal School for Daughters of Army Officers, is of a far more challenging design than the slightly earlier Kingswood School (page 194). It has irritated scholars, who have called it 'uncouth' and 'a confused jumble'. The reason for their annoyance is the undisciplined and almost brutal way in which the central part has combined its different architectural elements – the tower, the gable, the corner turret and the oriel. But the eccentricities are clearly deliberate, and show Wilson toying with the middle-of-the-century 'rogue' architecture made famous by S S Teulon at about the same time.

The range to the south-east was added by Habershon & Fawckner in 1884. The chapel to the south is by H Goodhart-Rendel, 1939.

North-west of Centre

LOCATION on the east side of Lansdown Road, further up from St Stephen's Church
ACCESS none

James Wilson 1856–58

North-west of Centre

James Wilson 1856–58

Kingswood School

This Methodist boys' school was founded by John Wesley in Kingswood, near Bristol. It is a traditional collegiate design in the early Tudor style – very much in fashion at the time – with symmetrical wings grouped around a central range in which a prominent tower with an oriel window above the entrance is flanked by two gables. Although it enjoys magnificent views over Bath, it fails to engage with the architecture of the city in the way that Oxford colleges do. This is a problem not only of location, but of expression – Wilson was the master of great, remote and, perhaps, bombastic designs. His proposal of 1837 for a university on Claverton Down to the south (where the present university stands) was joyless in the extreme.

Back at Kingswood School, the late-gothic-style chapel near the road entrance is by Gunton & Gunton, 1922.

LOCATION on the west side of Lansdown Road, higher up from the Royal School
ACCESS none

James Wilson 1851

James Wilson 1851

Beckford's Tower

In 1822 finances forced the eccentric William Beckford to sell his castle at Fonthill and move into two adjacent houses in Lansdown Place West and Lansdown Crescent. He became a familiar, if somewhat feared, figure on the Bath scene, riding everywhere in a cavalcade of mounted stewards with dogs, accompanied by a dwarf named Perro. The local press was full of speculation about the 'exotic and unholy rites' that it feared were being enacted behind the curtains of Lansdown Crescent.

Over the following years, Beckford once more felt the desire to transform the countryside – as he had at Fonthill – and created a picturesque walk through the virgin countryside up the hill from the rear of his home, terminating in the place where he built his Retreat or Tower, nearly 2 kilometres away on Lansdown Hill.

In the rear of his garden at no. 20 Lansdown Crescent, he built a tiny 'Islamic Pavilion' and, a little further up, an 'Embattled Gateway'. These two structures, both designed by Goodridge, have survived, although they are now inaccessible. The walk continued northwards across open country, but much of this is now built upon. To ensure his privacy, Beckford provided an alternative route for the public – and this too survives, as a grass path on the west side of Lansdown Road.

Just north of what is now Kingswood School, the route led past a plantation and some disused quarries, which pleased Beckford because they reminded him of the ruins of Rome. Then came a grotto tunnel and, finally, amidst exotic imported planting, the tower itself. Goodridge considered many options before settling for this then-fashionable Greek Revival interpretation, with its top part a cast-iron version of the Lysikrates Monument in Athens. At nearly 50 metres in height, the tower offered splendid views – from Bristol Channel in the west to the abandoned Fonthill in the east.

H E Goodridge 1827

H E Goodridge 1827

A small house was provided at the base of the tower, but after Beckford's death in 1844, the tower and grounds were given to the Rector of Walcot so that Beckford could be buried there – his tomb had originally been in the Abbey Cemetery (page 278). The architect Goodridge is also buried here.

The tower is now a museum.

North-west of Centre

LOCATION on the west side of Lansdown Hill, 2 kilometres north of Lansdown Crescent
ACCESS open to the public 14.00–17.00 Saturday, Sunday, Bank Holiday Mondays, April to October

H E Goodridge 1827

H E Goodridge 1827

North-east of Centre

Camden Crescent

Set high on the city's eastern slopes, looking over Bathwick, Camden Crescent is the first of Bath's great terraces that visitors see when arriving by the London train. Despite the closeness of Lansdown Crescent, it is the only great terrace visible from the eastern side of Bath. Its architecture is quite orthodox for its time. There are none of the tricks that Thomas Baldwin was trying out at the same time elsewhere in the city, and Camden Crescent even appears conventional when compared with the contemporary Lansdown Crescent (page 186) and Eveleigh's own Somerset Place (page 184). It is a piece of orthodox Palladian design. The rusticated base supports a giant order of engaged Corinthian columns, between which the first- and second-storey windows are placed.

Construction took place during the financial crises of the 1790s, and the scheme was also subject to landslips on the very difficult site. What we see today is not the complete project. For many years a north-eastern end stood isolated from the rest, but was eventually demolished.

Eveleigh originally intended that there should be a main crescent (comprising 22 units) forming a gentle curve, flanked by two straight ranges of five units each. In the event only the flanking range to the left was built.

The 'centre' of the terrace is now well off-centre, with only four units to its right. It has a pediment supported on five giant order Corinthian columns. This is, of course, bad practice in classical architecture – all temple fronts had an even number of columns and an odd number of bays in between – but the Palladian terrace was an adaptation of the classical formula to suit speculative developments. If, as here and elsewhere in Bath, the exact centre line marked the position of a party-wall between two houses, the obvious solution was to bend the rules and mask the line with a central column.

John Eveleigh 1788

John Eveleigh 1788

Within the pediment, the badly worn coat of arms with an elephant motif was that of Charles Pratt, Marquis of Camden. This motif is repeated in the single elephant head above each of the doorways.

Further to the north-east, along Camden Road, are Camden Terrace to the left and Lower Camden Place to the right, both distinguished designs of the 1820s. Walter Ison attributes them 'possibly' to Pinch the Elder. Somewhat further north-east are the four pairs of semi-detached houses called Claremont Place. Inscribed 1817, and again attributed to Pinch, it has been suggested that, on current evidence, they are the oldest surviving semi-detached houses in the country.

LOCATION Camden Crescent runs north-east from Lansdown Road, 400 metres north of its junction with George Street; a little further uphill on the left are Lansdown Crescent (page 186) and Somerset Place (page 184), with which it deserves comparison

John Eveleigh 1788

John Eveleigh 1788

Hedgemead View Housing

These terraces of houses on their steep hillside site effectively link the grand scale of John Eveleigh's Camden Crescent with the smaller-scale houses to the north-west.

They have developed the language of the local architecture by using blocks made of reconstituted stone, occasional grey courses, 'classical' tubular columns, and concrete-tiled roofs. The terraces have to cope with the steeply sloping site, and the lowest floor admits light from the north through pavement-level glazing.

Like most of the work by this practice, Hedgemead incorporates the highest standards in insulation and energy saving. The scheme won a Housing Design Award Commendation in 1987.

The parkland area of Hedgemead, to the south of the houses, was originally built up, and renowned as a centre of political agitation.

North-east of Centre

LOCATION on Upper Hedgemead Road, which runs from the south end of Camden Crescent alongside the tall retaining wall

Feilden Clegg Design 1984–87

Feilden Clegg Design 1984–87

Walcot Chapel (Walcot Methodist Church)

William Jenkins was an architect who became a minister; he specialised in the design of Methodist chapels, adjusting the applied architecture on each to its particular surroundings. At Walcot, apart from the fine Doric porch, the rest of the applied classicism is skin deep and two-dimensional. It is very dour, and not helped at all by a shallow pediment which is raised ('incorrectly', says Pevsner) above an attic of paired pilasters.

The building is a box, and the plain side and rear walls emphasise the point. On the north side is an old school entrance to the basement level.

Inside, there is a horseshoe-shaped gallery, but the chapel is not normally open for inspection.

North-east of Centre

LOCATION on London Road, just west of Cleveland Bridge; from Hedgemead, it is possible to cut through Hedgemead Park
ACCESS open for worship only

William Jenkins 1815–16

William Jenkins 1815–16

Cleveland Place

Cleveland Place is now a very busy traffic interchange and it is difficult to envisage it as Goodridge originally intended – as a dignified approach to his Cleveland Bridge.

The four-storey-façade theme of the east and west sides continues around both corners into London Road – the recurring motif is the three-part windows on each floor with blank panels on either side. It is still possible to see the attempts to match the façades on both sides (for example, no. 6 to the east matches no. 7 to the west). With its decorative treatment around the first and second floors, no. 9 was intended to be the central element of the west side.

The Dispensary on the east side (Goodridge, 1845) has a fine neoclassical façade with an Ionic portico, and sits well alongside his neoclassical bridge. It was built for the benefit of the 'sick poor from any parish in or near Bath'. An explanatory plaque on the outside gives a very good description of the building's history.

Walcot Parade on the north side, with its raised pavement, is of around 1770 and therefore predates Cleveland Place. When built, it faced open countryside and was very fashionable, although its individual units were not brought together into an architectural unity.

North-east of Centre

LOCATION the intersection where the A36 turns off the London Road to cross Cleveland Bridge

H E Goodridge 1829

H E Goodridge 1829

Cleveland Reach Houses

This small development of eight flats and maisonettes was built on a back-land site adjacent to Cleveland Bridge and facing the river. Its north, entrance side is domestic in character, with two large porches and wooden trellis work framing four entrances. By contrast, the river frontage is more 'modern' in character. The top two storeys are set back from the ground floor, creating a first-floor balcony, and the top storey is glazed and panelled, all within a thin frame of Bath stone blockwork.

The design incorporates a number of energy-saving features – including triple-glazed windows throughout – to achieve much higher standards of insulation than were required at the time. The large areas of glass facing the river act as passive solar collectors, and the two end maisonettes have 'trombe walls' which help to exploit the sun as a natural source of energy.

LOCATION the private river front can be seen from Cleveland Bridge; the entrance front is down the small drive 50 metres east of Cleveland Place (another example of this practice's work can be seen at Bridgemead, page 250, 150 metres away on the opposite side of Cleveland Bridge)

Feilden Clegg Design 1982

North-east of Centre

Feilden Clegg Design 1982

Cleveland Bridge

Built long after work had stopped on the uncompleted Bathwick Estate (see Great Pulteney Street, page 232), the Cleveland, or New, Bridge provided a second access to Bathwick from across the river. It has since been much strengthened to carry today's very busy motor traffic.

The bridge is supported on a series of parallel single-span iron arches of just over 30 metres, with lattice spandrels, but all this is virtually invisible to anyone other than the passengers on the tourist boats that pass beneath.

Far more conspicuous are the four toll houses that stand on the bridge's abutments. These are in a very fine Greek style, which was appropriate to the period (Sir Robert Smirke's British Museum in London was also under construction, and Harvey Lonsdale Elmes, architect of Liverpool's neoclassical St George's Hall, worked for Goodridge in the 1830s).

For its time, the bridge was an example of up-to-date and scholarly architecture combined with the latest engineering materials.

LOCATION just south of Cleveland Place; the river front on either side is private and inaccessible (boats can be joined at the Boating Station, Bathwick, 500 metres to the east)

H E Goodridge 1827

Snowhill Housing Development

The clean lines of Scandinavian architecture – very popular in the London County Council's housing of the 1950s – came to Bath at Snowhill, and gave the city its first tower block.

The steeply sloping site was made available by what was known at the time as a 'slum clearance programme'. The development's low-rise blocks were organised, like the city's grand Georgian terraces, along the contour lines, but with one block placed across the contours 'for contrast'.

The external staircases leading to the upper floors of the low blocks are a later addition. These blocks contain family flats, while the 12-storey tower block has one-bedroom flats.

The development is faced throughout in 100-mm-thick Bath stone ashlar, and its green copper roofs are a conspicuous feature of the city when seen from the surrounding hills.

LOCATION on the north side of the London Road, 200 metres east of Cleveland Place

Terence Snailum 1957

Terence Snailum 1957

Kensington Chapel

Because it now serves as a wine warehouse, this building, with its façade still blackened with age, hidden behind mature trees on the London Road, has escaped the attention of most commentators. It is, however, a fine piece of design, in which the chapel is the fully integrated centrepiece of a short terrace of housing.

The entrances to the chapel were at the sides, through the shallow arches. Its street elevation is composed with two tiers of three windows, the upper tier of which is brought together by a sill, pilasters and an entablature to suggest (depending on the way you want to read it) a colonnade interrupted by three arched windows, or three Venetian windows placed side by side.

The chapel is proof that applied decoration, when handled properly, can make very good architecture.

North-east of Centre

LOCATION head north-eastwards out of the city along the London Road; Kensington Chapel is about 500 metres beyond Cleveland Place on the right-hand side

John Palmer 1795

John Palmer 1795

Grosvenor Place

Set way out of the city on the London Road, Grosvenor Place was the northern range of an unrealised square of houses that was to have been built around Vauxhall Gardens next to the river – 'laid out with taste and elegance for the reception of Nobility, Gentry and the Public in general'. Although little remains of the gardens, their advertised features included an 'aviary, temple, labyrinth, swings, grotto ... saloon with organ' and 'alcoves'. The scheme was a failure, due partly to the inaccessibility of the site, and its low-lying ground.

In the centre of the one range of houses that survives is the building that was to have been a hotel, although never completed as such. Now converted into flats, and recently renovated, it is the centrepiece of the London Road frontage. Here once again, as at Somerset Place (page 184) and Camden Crescent (page 202), Eveleigh shows how inventive and unorthodox he could be. A giant Ionic order stands on a rusticated base, in the centre of which was the entrance through to Vauxhall Gardens (the porch is later). As at Camden Crescent, there is an odd number of columns, but here (even worse!) the central column stands above an opening. The decoration of the façade remains unfinished to this day.

LOCATION head north-eastwards out of the city along the London Road; Grosvenor Place is about 800 metres beyond Cleveland Place on the right-hand side (300 metres beyond the Kensington Chapel)

John Eveleigh 1791

John Eveleigh 1791

St Saviour's, Larkhall

The younger Pinch probably built this to the designs of his father, who died in 1827: it is certainly a direct successor of Pinch the Elder's St Mary's, Bathwick (page 244).

St Saviour's is a 'Commissioners Church', built under the Acts of Parliament of 1818 and 1824 that provided over a million pounds of public money for the construction of churches in poor neighbourhoods, where the control of the potentially unsettled population was considered most necessary.

The Commissioners, seeking an architecture that was cheap yet ecclesiastical, felt that the gothic idiom provided the most appropriate veneer. St Saviour's fulfils this brief convincingly. It provided places for over 1000 worshippers, of whom over 500 were non-fee-paying.

Externally, it is in the well-rehearsed perpendicular style of gothic, with a western tower, and a nave with tall side aisles and galleries. The three-bay chancel to the east was added by C E Davis in 1882.

LOCATION coming out of the city eastwards on the A4, just before Grosvenor Place on the right, St Saviour's Road forks left, leading to this conspicuous church
ACCESS open for worship only

John Pinch the Younger (to Pinch the Elder's design) 1829–32

John Pinch the Younger (to Pinch the Elder's design) 1829–32

Bathwick and Claverton

Pulteney Bridge

By the 1760s, Bathwick, to the east of the Avon, was an attractive prospect for development. William Johnstone Pulteney engaged Adam to build this bridge as a means of access to the east side, for in those days there was only one road crossing – the Old Bridge down near Southgate, which had been rebuilt a few years earlier.

We can guess at whether or not Adam relied on precedents for the design – Walter Ison convincingly cites Palladio's unexecuted design for the Rialto bridge in Venice, with three arched spans and an entrance portico at each end. The Palladio design also featured a large portico facing the river in the centre of the bridge; in the Pulteney Bridge this has become a large Venetian window. It is unique in Britain, and a lavish model was a principal exhibit in the Royal Academy's 1996 exhibition, *Living Bridges*.

Adam's design has been considerably altered. The original shopfronts were once contained within graceful arches, and the end pavilions had attached porticos facing outwards. Some of these pavilions have now lost their little domed roofs, and the one on the south-west corner has been moved towards the river to facilitate access to the Grand Parade. Despite recent attempts to clean up the bridge's outer faces, a mass of accretions still hang over the water on the north side.

At the time of writing, debate continues as to whether general vehicular traffic should be allowed to use the bridge. Pevsner, in 1958, wrote that it 'ought to be reserved for pedestrians as the much bigger Rialto Bridge is'. And so it should be.

Bathwick and Claverton

Robert Adam 1770

Robert Adam 1770

Argyle Street and Argyle Chapel

Pulteney Bridge leads into Argyle Street and what there is of the projected new town of Bathwick. This short street (it only runs as far as Laura Place, with its fountain) is hardly a grand entrance. Not only are the street frontages disappointing, but the two end gables which present themselves westwards across the river are built from rubble – what a magnificent composition they would have made if integrated with Pulteney Bridge to form an entrance portal to the new town.

After Grove Street, on the north side, is the portico of the Argyle Chapel. The church was founded in 1789, and H E Goodridge added the portico in 1821, although the upper part has been altered.

On the south side of the street, small steps lead down to the river beside the bridge (if you stop for a drink you can also get through via the Boater pub), where there is a new maze on the site of the Spring Gardens. The flood defence mechanism, with its raised platform, offers an excellent view of the river and the rugby ground on match days.

Back on Argyle Street, the corner chemist's has a lovely frontage, with large flasks of coloured water on display.

LOCATION the eastern extension of Pulteney Bridge, extending 150 metres to Laura Place

The (former) Prison

William Johnstone Pulteney's plans for his bridge and the future development of Bathwick required him to resite the city's prison, which was in an old church tower on the west side of the river, near the approach to the bridge.

Robert Adam, who had been closely involved with Pulteney's original plans, produced the initial design, but Atwood (the City Architect) prevailed, and his far more modest scheme was chosen.

It can now be seen close-to only from Grove Street, due to the recent domestic development on the other side. Bear in mind that the floor which is now at street level was designed to be the basement; it is not, because Grove Street was never raised up on vaults as had originally been intended. If we imagine the street at this higher level – above the present ground floor – the building is clearly a scholarly piece of Palladian design, with a heavily rusticated base and two storeys above. But the sombre and heavy treatment of its intended basement, with large voussoirs denoting strength and weight, gives it away as a prison.

The building has now been converted into flats.

LOCATION Grove Street runs north out of Argyle Street; the prison is 150 metres on the right. If you continue for another 450 metres down Grove Street and St John's Road, you will arrive at St John's Church (page 248), Bridgemead (page 250) and Cleveland Bridge (page 214)

Thomas Warr Atwood 1772

Bathwick and Claverton

Thomas Warr Atwood 1772

Great Pulteney Street and Laura Place

Following the construction of Pulteney Bridge, Robert Adam was commissioned in 1777 to prepare designs for the new town development of Bathwick. He prepared a number of options, including broad roads fanning out from circuses and crescents facing the river. The development was to cover the ground between what is now Cleveland Bridge to the north and the railway line to the south.

In the event, Adam's proposals were abandoned in favour of a design by Thomas Baldwin. Work started in 1788 and continued until finances collapsed in 1793. What did get built was not as impressive as it could have been, and despite some later additions to the scheme, there are still some strangely short streets off Great Pulteney Street which were never completed.

After Pulteney Bridge and Argyle Street comes Laura Place, where Baldwin's work begins. Lozenge-shaped in plan, its four façades are identical, and the eight corners gently emphasised. The central fountain is recent. Johnstone Street to the south is unfinished.

Great Pulteney Street itself has grand proportions – 335 metres long by 31 metres wide, with all the opportunities for gestures that such an urban scale affords. But the architecture of the terraces that face the street fails to do justice to these opportunities. The north side is divided into two by an incomplete side road (Sunderland Street). Its two long terraces use pediments and occasional pilasters to gather themselves into some sort of composition, but their subtlety is overwhelmed by their weakness.

On the south side, two side roads allow a more appropriate gesture: the centre block between Edward Street and William Street has some presence, with a grand order of pilasters.

Peter Smithson called the details of Great Pulteney Street 'virtuoso stuff', and in some parts this is true. But the proportions of the street are

Thomas Baldwin 1788–93

Thomas Baldwin 1788–93

too magnificent for Bath, and although the Holburne Museum at its eastern end is a fine building in itself, it is not sufficiently imposing to terminate such a grand vista. Nor, for that matter, is the vista terminated well in the opposite direction. The Laura Place fountain hardly interrupts the view, which fizzles out beyond Pulteney Bridge. For something that started so optimistically with the construction of the country's only 'inhabited bridge', the Bathwick development has more than its fair share of failed opportunities.

Bathwick and Claverton

LOCATION Great Pulteney Street extends from Laura Place to the Holburne Museum

Thomas Baldwin 1788–93

Thomas Baldwin 1788–93

Holburne Museum

Thomas Baldwin proposed that a pleasure garden and hotel (a two-storey building with a central portico facing down the street) should be placed at the end of Great Pulteney Street. Following his bankruptcy in 1793, Masters took over the scheme. He added a rusticated basement to Baldwin's hotel design, making it into a three-storey composition (whose façade, incidentally, is similar to that of Baldwin's Guildhall of 1776, see page 120).

When built, the rusticated base was extended in wings each side of the main building, and there were five bays of windows on each of the two upper floors. In 1836, Pinch the Younger added the attic storey.

After the decline in popularity of pleasure gardens, the Sydney Hotel (or Tavern), as it was called, became a college; it was acquired for its present use in 1915. Sir Reginald Blomfield adapted it as a museum, and in doing so united the first and second floors internally and refaced the façade, omitting the second-floor windows and creating the much taller *piano nobile* windows that we see today. He also provided the poor rear elevation in place of what had been a delightful garden loggia. The small playfully decorated teashop attracts visitors and provides a distant reminder of the way things were.

LOCATION at the end of Great Pulteney Street
ACCESS Monday to Saturday (closed mid-December to mid-February, and Monday from mid-February to Easter); entrance charge

Bathwick and Claverton

Charles Harcourt Masters 1796

Bathwick and Claverton

Charles Harcourt Masters 1796

Sydney Place

Only two sides of Sydney Gardens' elongated hexagon are fronted by Georgian terraces, and only that to the north of Great Pulteney Street is part of the original development by Baldwin. It is a simple three-storey design, with slight articulation of the centre and ends (the pediment at the north end is missing). The central feature is four bays wide. This implies a classical portico with an odd number of columns, one of which is on the centre line – John Eveleigh had a similar problem at about the same time in Camden Crescent (page 202).

The handsome terraces of Daniel Street behind the north range were built by Pinch in 1810. They lead north to busy Bathwick Street, built by Baldwin in the 1790s.

The south range of Sydney Place by Pinch has four storeys, but succeeds where other four-storey compositions fail because of the way it steps, unit by unit, down the slope – see also Pinch's Cavendish Place of the same year (page 172). This stepping gives the architecture sufficient strength and disposes of the need for central and end pediments, which would have been superfluous here at Sydney Place, and have never been convincing when grafted on to a four-storey terrace.

On the east end, there is a handsome porch with a conservatory above. A similar feature is placed on the corner at the city end, to acknowledge the junction with Great Pulteney Street.

LOCATION if you stand facing the Holburne Museum, the Pinch range is to your right, the older Baldwin range to your left (Bathwick Street, which leads to Cleveland Bridge, is at the end of Baldwin's range)

Thomas Baldwin 1792; John Pinch the Elder 1808

Thomas Baldwin 1792; John Pinch the Elder 1808

Sydney Gardens

The axis of Great Pulteney Street was split at its east end to form an elongated hexagon of roads around these pleasure gardens to the rear of the Sydney Hotel. Features of the gardens (covering some 6 hectares) included waterfalls, thatched pavilions, alcoves, 'vistoes' and a labyrinth. They were originally ringed by a carriage ride, but all this has now been fragmented by walls, hedges, and some more recent houses on the south side.

The Kennet and Avon Canal (page 242), in 1799, and the railway (page 158), in 1841, were constructed through the gardens, and in both cases the bridge crossings provided were in the best possible taste. The temple beside the railway bridge dates from 1909, and the year afterwards, the Corporation acquired the site. It is now a public park, with the promenade alongside the railway line still a pleasant feature.

Very little remains of the pleasure gardens, which in their heyday attracted 4000 visitors a day. The main axis from the hotel (now the Holburne Museum) to Sydney House to the north-east is scarcely evident as such today.

LOCATION the main entrance to the park is at the end of Bathwick Street, or the northern end of Baldwin's Sydney Place; it can also be entered by a small gate on the canal
ACCESS open at all times

Bathwick and Claverton

Charles Harcourt Masters 1795

Charles Harcourt Masters 1795

The Kennet and Avon Canal

The canal was opened for navigation from the Avon at Bath to the Thames at Reading in 1810, but three decades later the Great Western Railway proved a fierce competitor, eventually buying the canal in 1851.

One century later the Kennet and Avon fell derelict, but the entire route was reopened in the 1990s as a result of concerted voluntary action.

The canal is now one of the city's greatest public assets: from Bathampton to the east, it passes through countryside into the fringes of Bath's Georgian development, passing through two short tunnels with ornate portals as it cuts through Sydney Gardens. Many original features remain, including the delicate iron bridges in Sydney Gardens and the handsome Canal House which straddles the water above one of the tunnels.

There are marvellous views of the Abbey to the right before the Widcombe flight of locks begins. The penultimate lock is the deepest on any inland waterway in Britain (it replaced two locks when Widcombe's one-way road system was built).

The canal is an architectural perambulation in its own right.

LOCATION if following the sequence in this book, the best entrance is through the small white gate in Sydney Gardens; other principal points of access are where the canal joins the River Avon at Thimble Mill near Widcombe, and at the northern tunnel portal on Beckford Road, on the A36 in Bathwick (the George Inn at Bathampton is a very pleasant half-hour's walk away)

Bathwick and Claverton

John Rennie 1799

John Rennie 1799

St Mary's, Bathwick

Bath was well served with a number of good Gothic Revival churches, of which St Mary's is the finest. An earlier St Mary's church stood beside the river near what is now St John the Baptist (page 248). Its derelict Burial Chapel survives.

The present St Mary's has a tall west tower of three stages with engaged octagonal buttresses – like the Abbey. The nave is of five bays, with lower side aisles. Externally, it is pinnacled and crenellated everywhere.

The tall interior, unlike St Michael's in Broad Street (page 60), still has its gallery, although it is hard to believe that, until 1866, the pews faced west. There are fine plaster vaults to the nave and aisles. The chancel was built by G E Street in 1873 – his only venture into Bath.

A few metres up Bathwick Hill, beside the church, is Raby Place, built by John Pinch the Elder from 1818 to 1825. It carries Pinch's unmistakable hallmarks – verandas on the first floor and quadrants in the mouldings as the units step down the hill (because the slope is so steep, central and end pediments would have been unthinkable here). Together with Pinch's contemporary Cavendish Crescent, Raby Place marks the end of the vigorous period of Georgian terrace construction that had started a century earlier.

LOCATION St Mary's is the conspicuous church 200 metres south of the Holburne Museum; Raby Place starts 50 metres south of the church. Goodridge's Fiesole (page 252) and the university (page 256) are further up Bathwick Hill)

ACCESS during times of worship only

John Pinch the Elder 1817–20

John Pinch the Elder 1817–20

Hampton Row

The area to the north of Bathwick Street is an extensive turn-of-the-century suburban development in the grounds of Bathwick Villa, which was where nos. 13 and 14 Forester Road now stand. At the end of Forester Road is the charming Victorian Boating Station.

Further to the north are some Georgian survivors – Hampton Row, a humble terrace of cottages, is a very good demonstration of how the architectural language of grand terraces was adapted for smaller buildings. When built, it followed the line of the canal (page 242), which was then diverted to make way for the railway (page 158). Brunel's new retaining wall was constructed alongside the canal's new alignment.

Nearby is Rose Cottage (Feilden Clegg Design, 1991) and adjacent to this are steps leading down to the old open-air Georgian pleasure baths beside the Avon (now closed and private property).

LOCATION take the A36 exit at the roundabout at the end of Bathwick Street and turn left immediately, just before the railway and canal bridges, along Beckford Gardens; Hampton Row is at the end (from the end of Hampton Row a footbridge over the railway leads up to the canal)

St John the Baptist, Bathwick

Bathwick Street is now a busy traffic route. Nos. 1–21 on the north-east side are by Thomas Baldwin, 1790. At the northern end of the street, St John the Baptist, hidden amongst the trees just to the east of Cleveland Bridge, could almost be called two churches.

The original structure (itself a replacement for a medieval church) was a satisfying composition, with its own chancel. Although a tower was added in 1865, it was still too small; Sir Arthur Blomfield built a new marquee-like nave on its south side in 1871, relegating the old nave to the status of north aisle. Blomfield's church is a vigorous example of the High Victorian Gothic church architecture that had been established so forcefully 20 years earlier by William Butterfield at All Saints' Church in Margaret Street, London.

Of special note in the interior are the painted Stations of the Cross (c.1900 by Edward Frampton) and the Baptistery. The sunken floor here – apparently to allow for baptism by total immersion – has a mosaic pattern depicting a net and fishes.

In the disgracefully unkempt and fenced-off grounds is an old Burial Chapel which belonged to St Mary's, Bathwick (page 244).

On the other side of Bathwick Street, just to the right of the new flats, is a decorative archway. This is 'Pinch's folly', built by Pinch the Younger's son William as an entrance to his builder's yard. It gained significance after Leonora Ison's illustration of it appeared at the front of her husband's book in 1948. Her illustration also served as a reference during the gateway's subsequent restoration.

LOCATION principal entrance off St John's Road, which meets Bathwick Street at Cleveland Bridge (page 214)
ACCESS during times of worship only

C E Giles 1861; Sir Arthur Blomfield 1871

C E Giles 1861; Sir Arthur Blomfield 1871

Bridgemead

This nursing and residential home with day centre for the frail elderly occupies a quiet riverside site. It is set back from St John's Road, providing an open court for car parking.

Externally, it effectively combines a modern range of materials while acknowledging the context of traditional building in Bath.

Internally, the home is planned in two wings placed around a well-lit and protected communal space. One of the key design strategies was the careful and disciplined grading of internal space – from the public areas, through the semi-private shared areas, to the most intimate and secluded private rooms.

LOCATION at the northern end of St John's Road, which runs from Argyle Street (as Grove Street) to Cleveland Bridge; another example of the practice's work is at Cleveland Reach (page 212), 150 metres away on the opposite side of Cleveland Bridge
ACCESS none

Feilden Clegg Design 1992

Feilden Clegg Design 1992

Bathwick Hill and Fiesole

Bathwick Hill offers a fine collection of private houses which demonstrate the evolution of nineteenth-century fashion – from the austerity of the Georgian era, through the Italianate influence that was especially strong in Bath from the 1830s, to the eclectic picturesque of the mid-century.

It was here that Goodridge built Montebello for himself in 1828, in sharp contrast to Pinch the Elder's Raby Place at the foot of the hill. Twenty years later, and further down the hill, Goodridge built Fiesole, along with its neighbours La Casetta and Casa Bianca. Not only did these houses carry Italian names, but they were also Goodridge's consistent and well-observed interpretations of Italian villa architecture. He later moved out of Montebello and made Fiesole his home. Although its two-storey loggia remains intact, many of its features have been altered – but who can complain? It now serves as the city's Youth Hostel, where members can enjoy a little piece of Goodridge for themselves.

Elsewhere on Bathwick Hill, Oakwood of 1830 is also by Goodridge, with later additions. The octagonal Spa Villa at no. 9 is by Pinch, 1820.

Bathwick and Claverton

LOCATION St Mary's Bathwick (page 244) is at the bottom of Bathwick Hill, which is also on the bus route to the university (page 256)
ACCESS all private dwellings; YHA members have access to Fiesole

H E Goodridge 1848

H E Goodridge 1848

Claverton Down Gospel Hall

Although now slightly overgrown and in need of attention, this is a delightful representative of end-of-the-century 'free' architecture so rarely seen in Bath. The only other examples from this period are St Michael's Church House in Walcot Street (page 80) and some of the now crumbling (or demolished) turn-of-the-century schools in the city.

With rendered walls, wide mullioned windows and strong corner buttresses, the hall is reminiscent of Voysey – although he was not to build in the area until 1909 (page 286). Notice how the buttresses protrude through the roof line, ending in two kneeling angels facing outwards.

Bathwick and Claverton

LOCATION at the top of Widcombe Hill on the north side, near the university
ACCESS none

T B Silcock 1896

T B Silcock 1896

The University of Bath

The open fields on the top of Claverton Down had already been chosen as the site for an academic institution when, in 1837, abortive work began on Queen's College – a theological university to the designs of James Wilson.

The development plan for a new University of Technology at Claverton, to be formed out of the Bristol College of Advanced Technology, was published in 1965. It showed the development's principal discipline: a linear, extendable 'mall' with teaching schools either side, all raised up one storey to leave services and traffic at ground level.

The Buchanan Report of 1963 had advocated 'traffic architecture', in which pedestrians are segregated vertically from traffic, and it is not surprising that Colin Buchanan was traffic consultant to the new university. He argued for high-quality landscape design to support these first-floor pedestrian 'decks', and here in Bath they were successful – but in the majority of social housing developments where the principle was adopted they were a disaster.

Much of the original concept survives intact, but – true to the philosophy of expansion – there are some later additions of note.

The 6 East building, by the celebrated British modern architects Alison and Peter Smithson, lays down a benchmark for architecture that combines concrete with the traditional material of Bath. Its intriguingly skewed interior is a budget-priced statement of the couple's doctrine – all the service ducts and lintels over doors are exposed. It serves well as the university's School of Architecture, and this author's base.

The Smithsons also designed a number of other buildings on the campus, including the unfinished theatre in the grounds of the Arts Barn. This centre for the arts is badly needed by the university and it is to be hoped that at some point in the future it will be completed.

RMJM & Partners 1971; A + P Smithson 1988

Bathwick and Claverton

RMJM & Partners 1971; A + P Smithson 1988

The University Library, still in the centre of the RMJM scheme, was extended in 1996 by the Alec French Partnership. Its fashionably applied tension structure dominates the axis down the steps towards the well-landscaped grounds and lake.

Bathwick and Claverton

LOCATION can be reached on foot up Bathwick Hill or North Hill, or by bus 18 from the bus station, via Laura Place; the 6 East building is right by the bus stop ACCESS to the parade and grounds only

RMJM & Partners 1971; A + P Smithson 1988

Bathwick and Claverton

RMJM & Partners 1971; A + P Smithson 1988

The American Museum (Claverton Manor)

Set on the top of Claverton Down and commanding magnificent views over the Avon Valley, this house for John Vivian was built by Wyatville (who was King George IV's architect) to replace an earlier Jacobean structure in the village below.

Built in local stone, it is in neoclassical style, with a chaste east front with Ionic pilasters and pediment, and a southern façade with two full-height bays looking out over the valley. In 1828 Vivian's son added the screen wall by the drive and a picture gallery. In 1850 it was sold to the Skrine family of nearby Warleigh Manor, whose arms remain on the south front pediment.

Two Americans bought the manor in 1958 and, anxious to promote links between the West Country and America, founded the American Museum in 1961 – the first museum of Americana established outside the USA. The main collection, housed in a series of rooms furnished in the American tradition, includes a display of Shaker furniture.

In the grounds, the separate bookshop and gallery is a piece of joyless stripped classicism signed by Ian McCallum and John A Roberts, 1986.

LOCATION starting from beside the university's sports fields, The Avenue leads to the museum, which is signposted. Alternatively, it can be approached from the valley below. Take the A36 (or the canal towpath out of Bath – an excellent walk) to Claverton, and head straight uphill ACCESS open daily afternoons, except Mondays, late March to early November; occasional weekends up to Christmas. Hours for the museum and grounds differ – given the location it is best to check. Telephone 01225 460503

Sir Jeffry Wyatville 1820

Sham Castle

High up on Claverton Down, this ornamental piece was built by Ralph Allen to be seen from the east windows of his Town House (page 144), and as an advertisement for the stone from his quarries. Like many eighteenth-century follies, it is merely a clever piece of stage design, and a forlorn disappointment when seen close-to – its battlemented walls seem just thick enough to stand up.

But it must have looked dramatic in Allen's day, when it was not surrounded by so many trees. Now floodlights lend their own drama at night-time.

LOCATION can be reached by footpath from the university; it is situated just after the timber footbridge over Quarry Road (on leaving Sham Castle, more footpaths lead downhill, across North Road, offering fine views of the city)
ACCESS free access at all times

attributed to Richard Jones 1762

South of the River

Commercial and Industrial Developments, Lower Bristol Road

The inner fringe area between the south bank of the Avon and the railway has a number of notable recent commercial and industrial developments.

Just to the west of Churchill Bridge are refurbished riverside warehouses in commercial use, including Waterfront House and the offices of renowned building engineers, Buro Happold.

Further west on the same side, opposite the Green Park Tavern and Westmoreland Road, Aaron Evans Associates' car showroom is the most spectacular contribution to the city's portfolio of modern architecture, with its lightweight roof folded into sharp angular forms that are quite appropriate to its busy roadside setting. The same practice's speculative development of 12 office units just to the east (Riverside Court, 1989) uses the same roof motif, but in a less dynamic way. It comprises two parallel wings either side of a parking court.

On the south side of the Lower Bristol Road, opposite the car showroom, is another estate of office development grouped around a central parking court. The Square (Ian Penrose, 1992) also incorporates a refurbished Great Western Railway goods shed.

LOCATION from the city centre, cross the river at Churchill Bridge and follow the Lower Bristol Road

Widcombe Primary School

Similar in many respects to the practice's earlier school on Julian Road (page 168), this single-storey structure replaces a demolished three-storey Edwardian building that stood at the north end of the site. Many features of the old building have been retained – including the bell tower – and its foundations can be seen within the present school grounds.

The new building is entered underneath the 'prow' at its eastern end. It forms an L in plan, with a hall to the west, connecting with some retained accommodation, and the classroom range to the north. Poor ground conditions meant that much material had to be removed, and these classrooms are sunk well down. They are organised in pairs on the road side of a corridor spine which gives access to the playground behind. Natural ventilation is drawn by duct from the playground and exhausted through the vents in the roof.

The school is faced with recycled Bath stone and, like St Andrew's School (page 168), has some interesting windows on its public front.

LOCATION on the east side of Pulteney Road, just north of the Widcombe one-way system. The Magistrates Court (page 152) is 300 metres further north on Pulteney Road

Nealon Tanner Partnership 1996

Nealon Tanner Partnership 1996

Dolemeads Estate

As in other British urban centres, there was much poor-quality housing within the city of Bath at the end of the nineteenth century. Following the Housing of the Working Classes Act of 1890, the council was empowered to clear areas that it designated as 'insanitary', and replace them with new housing.

The low-lying Dolemeads area was prone to flooding from the river, and by the end of the nineteenth century had become a slum. Starting in 1901, the ground in the area was raised, and the first seven council houses of the new Dolemeads Estate were built in Archway Street, followed by those in Excelsior Street. The improvement in living conditions was dramatic.

Atypically for Bath, the homes were built in red brick – a more suburban-scale development in the same material appeared in Powlett Road, Bathwick at the same time. Dolemeads survives today as a welcome reminder of the pioneer years of municipal enterprise, easily visible from trains crossing the railway viaduct in whose shadow it stands.

South of the River

LOCATION just behind Widcombe Primary School, on the east side of Pulteney Road. The Magistrates Court (page 152) is 300 metres further north on Pulteney Road

1901–10

1901–10

Widcombe Crescent and Terrace

The main concave frontage of the crescent faces the old turnpike road; its convex rear faces downhill towards the city. This is unique for a Bath crescent.

The street frontage brings each pair of units together into a composition that is plain but sensitive and effective. At the centre of each pair the two doorways are collected beneath a shallow recessed arch. The principal rooms face towards the view.

Further uphill in Widcombe Terrace the front doors are also to the rear, with the back doors to the street. This presents a problem: how do you gain access to the private garden from the same side as the front door? At Widcombe (because of the slope) this is achieved by means of a pavement that bridges over the entrance to the garden.

It has been suggested that this group marks the beginning of the end for the Palladian terrace, as developers began to turn their backs upon recognisable urban forms in a desire to relate their houses more individually to the landscape.

LOCATION the bottom of Widcombe Hill is 200 metres east of the small footbridge behind the railway station; Widcombe Crescent is 300 metres up the hill on the right

Charles Harcourt Masters 1805

Charles Harcourt Masters 1805

Widcombe Manor

Dating from just before the start of Queen Square, the rebuilding of this manor in a then separate village outside Bath marks a high point for pre-Wood domestic architecture. The design cannot be credited to an architect with certainty: the local pre-Wood generation, on the basis of smaller works in Bath, did not on the whole go in for such refinements.

The fluted Ionic pilasters, the windows with architraves, and the heavy keystones are similar to, say, the south front of Talman's Chatsworth House in Derbyshire (1686). The west front, with its bay window, is a sympathetic addition of the nineteenth century. There is a lovely Palladian garden house in the grounds.

St Thomas à Becket's Church, just over the garden wall, was started in the late fifteenth century and is therefore slightly older than the Abbey.

This is all rural village architecture – and just under a kilometre from the city's mainline railway station.

LOCATION go up Widcombe Hill and fork right into Church Street for both buildings; (Claverton Down Gospel Hall, page 254, and the university, page 256, can also be approached up Widcombe Hill)

1727

Prior Park Buildings

This terrace stands on the west side of Prior Park Road, which used to be the course of Ralph Allen's railway from his quarries to his wharf near the river at Thimble Mill.

It is set back from the road, with the Lyn Brook and gardens in front. The stream, walkways and planting between the houses and the road provide increased peace and privacy.

The terrace itself is set uphill from the road and is handsomely composed. Although the window rhythm of its rusticated ground floor is different from that of the floors above, the architecture is strong enough to deal with it. Most of the terrace is three storeys high, but the wide pedimented centre has four, the top one of which is masterfully contained by the pediment itself.

LOCATION Prior Park Road (A3062) starts at the same spot as Widcombe Hill; the terrace is 100 metres up on the right

John Pinch the Elder 1825

The Abbey Cemetery

The Scot Loudon made cemetery design into a science, and published widely on the subject. To this day, the Bath cemetery, along with another in Cambridge, remains a clear exposition of Loudon's beliefs. He wrote that cemeteries should be in airy, well-lit locations on high ground, and systematically laid out with a hierarchy of gravel walks and grass paths, although not too formal looking that they would deter the visitors who came to enjoy their picturesque landscaping. At the Abbey Cemetery, a carriage road runs along the side of the plots, which are laid out on a north–south grid centred on the small chapel.

Today, most of the monuments are overgrown, providing an excellent wild habitat, but the paths are still kept clear. It is a very tranquil place to visit, and offers fine views over the city.

The Cemetery Chapel of the same period is by G P Manners. It is in bad shape, and at the time of writing its future is uncertain.

South of the River

LOCATION go up Prior Park Road (A3062); the cemetery is 600 metres on the right, at the junction with Perrymead Hill
ACCESS the grounds are open, but the chapel is inaccessible at present

John Claudius Loudon 1843

The Cemetery, with distant view of Bath.

John Claudius Loudon 1843

Prior Park

Ralph Allen acquired the Bath stone quarries at Combe Down in 1726, but needed to reassure builders (especially those in London) that the material was suitable for grand constructions. This prompted him to build his new mansion out of the stone, right next to the quarry, and commanding views down Widcombe towards the city. Pevsner has called it 'the most ambitious and the most complete re-creation of Palladio's villas on English soil'.

Wood, who had built Allen's town house (page 144) in 1727, was also engaged on the new house, until a row split the two men in 1748. His original conception was perfectly symmetrical, with the mansion in the centre flanked on both sides by 'Wings of Offices', as in a Palladian villa in the Veneto. But here the wings were slightly inclined towards each other in plan, forming a shallow angular 'crescent'. It has been suggested that this was the inspiration for the great urban crescents of Bath that came a little later.

Following Wood's dismissal, Richard Jones (the clerk of works) was engaged, and he altered the scheme's symmetry.

Prior Park became a Catholic college in 1830 (the year of Catholic emancipation), when the east and west wings were altered. It was gutted by fire in 1836; in 1924 it became a boys' school, and was gutted once again in 1990.

What remains is a far cry from Wood's conception. The main mansion survives, with its entrance to the south, a similar but grander front with portico looking down on the vista to the north, and an especially fine Palladian east front. The stairs on the north front were added by H E Goodridge in 1830 when it became a college.

The magnificent church of St Paul's on the site of the old west wing was begun by J J Scoles in 1844, but funds ran out during construction

John Wood the Elder 1735

John Wood the Elder 1735

and it fell into ruins. Work was restarted, and it was consecrated in 1882. It has an exceptionally fine Roman-style interior.

The grounds, within a steeply sided valley, are a fine example of the English Landscape movement. They were laid out between 1759 and 1764 by 'Capability' Brown. Features that can be seen today include the 'Wilderness' just north-west of the house (designed by the poet Alexander Pope in 1740) and, further downhill from the mansion, a decorative 'Palladian Bridge' built in the 1750s, based on a drawing by Palladio. Over the main span is a slender enclosed colonnade, with a pavilion at each end.

Following years of neglect, the gardens were restored by the National Trust and opened to the public in 1996. The recommended route sweeps past the garden front of the mansion and offers breathtaking views of the valley and the bridge.

LOCATION visitors are encouraged to leave their cars behind and walk or cycle (Ralph Allen Drive is very steep!) or take public transport (bus 2 or 4 from the bus station); if travelling by car, take Prior Park Road south from the city for 1.5 kilometres – the entrance is on the left, but there is no car parking on site or nearby

ACCESS open Wednesday to Monday (closed Christmas Day, Boxing Day and New Year's Day) 12.00–17.30 (entrance charge; discount available on presentation of public transport ticket)

John Wood the Elder 1735

South of the River

John Wood the Elder 1735

Combe Down Primary School

Underneath Combe Down there are many stone quarries. The unstable ground in the area was one of the reasons why Avon County Council chose this Finnish, lightweight 'off-the-peg' timber building – other reasons were the excellent insulation qualities it offered and the fact that it was substantially cheaper than a conventional brick building.

All of the walls are from round logs of Finnish pine, which are left exposed outside and in, creating an intimate environment appropriate to the building's function.

Nearby is Holy Trinity Church, Combe Down (H E Goodridge, 1835). It is another of Pevsner's 'crazy' churches (in company with St Michael's, Broad Street, page 60, and St Stephen's, Lansdown, page 190). He uses the word here to refer to the west tower, implying that it was inventive and not at all scholarly. But, when built, the church was a simple box-like building, rather like the Commissioners' Church (see St Saviour's, Larkhall, page 222). The chancel and aisles were added later in 1884 – 'far too well-mannered to compete with the tower' says Pevsner.

South of the River

LOCATION take the A3062 south of the city; just after Prior Park cross over the junction into The Avenue for the primary school and church ACCESS the school is gated; no public access to the grounds

1990

1990

Lodge Style

What is now Prior Park College (page 280) was built out of the local stone. So too was Lodge Style – for Thomas Sturge Cotterell, owner of St Winifred's Quarry.

This comparatively small house is a fairly late example of Voysey's work, and the only one in the area (which, in general, has very few survivors from the early twentieth century). It is a low and humble composition for an architect whose reputation was already well established, and it is clear that Cotterell cut costs during the design process. The house is arranged around four sides of a small central courtyard; the only two-storey element is a tower in the north-west corner, adjacent to the battlemented entrance on the north side.

LOCATION from Combe Down, proceed eastwards along North Road; after 500 metres take Shaft Road to the right. The driveway to Lodge Style is on the left
ACCESS none

C F A Voysey 1909

C F A Voysey 1909

West of the City

Royal Victoria Park

The notion of picturesque landscaping had first arrived in Bath with William Beckford's private walk up to his tower on Lansdown (see page 196). In contrast, this new park was a public enterprise, built on common land to the west of the Circus.

The main entrance is on the west side of Marlborough Buildings. Its Greek Revival entrance gates and the 'Gothic Farm House' nearby are both by Davis. The farmhouse – a *cottage orné* – with its heavy barge-boards and picturesque silhouette, is now two cottages, in residential use. The three-sided obelisk near the entrance was erected by G P Manners in 1837.

The park's eastern part, on the other side of Marlborough Lane, was built on the fields immediately south of the Royal Crescent. At its eastern end, and very close to Queen Square and the Royal Circus, is the new Royal Pavilion (MWT Architects/Brian Bishop Architects, 1992), serving the tennis courts and bowling greens. With its overhanging eaves, timber and green-painted steel, it is a creditable addition to the park. Its lowest level is set back, offering shade to spectators, while its first-floor is cantilevered forward, with wide windows for the benefit of the restaurant customers inside.

LOCATION Marlborough Lane is at the west end of the Royal Crescent; the Royal Pavilion can be reached through the park's eastern entrance, just behind the north-west corner of Queen Square
ACCESS the park is permanently open

laid out by Edward Davis 1829

laid out by Edward Davis 1829

Partis College

Described by Neil Jackson as 'the most striking example of Greek Revival architecture in the West Country', this is not in fact a college, but a group of 30 almshouses, endowed to provide accommodation for 'gentlewomen of reduced circumstances' – a function it still fulfils.

When built, it commanded views over the Newbridge fields, much of which were owned by the Partis family, but it is now in suburbia, hiding from a busy A-road behind thick planting. Neither this, nor the disappointing approach from the south-east, do justice to the dignity of the architecture.

It is, like a college, a symmetrical composition around three sides of a court. In the centre, behind the hexastyle (six-columned) Ionic portico is the chapel (the interior by Gilbert Scott, 1862, is a contrast in Italian gothic), and this is flanked by the ranges of four-roomed houses, each with its own white front door. Each range is terminated by pavilions with Doric pilasters.

LOCATION on the Newbridge Road (A431) 2.5 kilometres west of Bath
ACCESS none – it jealously guards its privacy and security

Samuel and Philip Flood Page 1827

Samuel and Philip Flood Page 1827

When the high-tech out-of-town shed arrived in Bath, even the GRP (glass reinforced plastic) panels deferred to the colour of Bath stone.

Herman Miller, the furniture manufacturer, wanted additional premises close to its existing factory on the banks of the River Avon. The main requirement of the new building was that it should be highly flexible, combining the functions of office space, factory and storage in a way that could be altered at any time in the future.

The GRP panels of the façade are arranged in two tiers, surmounted by a curved parapet. Each of the panels is joined to its neighbour with a flexible Neoprene gasket, so that the configuration of the wall can be changed easily by rearranging the doors and glazed or blank panels.

The most successful external feature of the building is the full-height glazed area facing the river. Immediately in front of this is a well-land-scaped seating area for staff – a delightful spot in summer.

Nicholas Grimshaw designed a similar building for Herman Miller in nearby Chippenham in 1983.

On the other side of the river, just over the footbridge, the other Herman Miller building is by Yorke Rosenberg Mardall, 1967.

Still on the riverside, but further downstream (or west) off Brassmill Lane, is the Rotork Controls Factory by Leonard Manasseh Partnership, 1966.

LOCATION on Brassmill Trading Estate, Brassmill Lane, just south of the A4 Newbridge Road, 2 kilometres out of town (turn left down Station Road); can also be approached on foot along the north bank of the Avon

Terry Farrell and Nicholas Grimshaw 1977

Terry Farrell and Nicholas Grimshaw 1977

Public Housing, Twerton

The estates at the far west end of developed Bath are excellent examples of postwar planning strategies and industrialised building techniques. Along Newton Road, Day Crescent on the north side has 'Cornish Units' of precast concrete panels with mansard roofs (1949). On the south side, the 'BISF' steel-panelled houses of Cleeve Green (1949) face a car-free open green space.

The Whiteway Estate just to the south is a typical piece of inter-war municipal development. It was planned on a series of concentric rings, originally leaving an open playing field in the centre. The units on Haycombe Drive, and the roads to its immediate north, were designed by the City Engineer's Department, based on standard layouts published by the Government. Built from 1936 on, their internal planning represented the latest thinking of the time.

LOCATION Twerton is just south of the A36, 2 kilometres west of the city; Newton Road is the westerly extension of the High Street

1936–49

West of the City

1936–49

Index

Bath: an architectural guide

Bath: an architectural guide